The Pocket ALEISTER CROWLEY

Trident Press
Boulder, CO

Edited by Jake Dirnberger
& Nathaniel Kennon Perkins

Published by Trident Press
940 Pearl St.
Boulder, CO 80302

tridentcafe.com

ISBN: 978-0-999-2499-8-7

The Pocket
ALEISTER CROWLEY

Contents

Editor's Introduction

Dangerous, mysterious, obscure, powerful, amoral: these qualities perhaps describe Aleister Crowley the person as well as they do the force of magick itself. Indeed, few modern figures have captured the imagination in such a way to place them so far beyond designations of good and evil. In his life, Crowley was called "the most evil man in Britain," but despite that (or perhaps also because of it) his popularity persists well into the present. Crowley was a revolutionary occult thinker, whose works are still widely read and whose famous *Thoth* Tarot deck is among the most popular, unique, and symbolically rich decks of our time. Near the end of the 19th century, Crowley was initiated into the Golden Dawn tradition, a system of ritual magic inspired primarily by Hermeticism,

Gnosticism, Freemasonry, and Kabbalah. However, he eventually broke from the Golden Dawn over matters of authority. Channeling his own inspiration from the spirit *Aiwass*, he revolutionized magick by replacing the focus upon the individual magician. "Every man and woman is a star," Crowley tells us in the first line of his famous *Liber Al Legis*, or *the Book of the Law*, "Every number is infinite, there is no difference." In other words, we are the mystery to be solved and the light to be sought. Several lines later, it is stated that, "The Khabs is in the Khu, not the Khu in the Khabs," or, in other words, the universe is in us, not us in the universe.

The Book of the Law introduces the meta-ideal that drives Crowley's main magickal project—the ushering of humanity into a new age, the Aeon of Horus. For Crowley, there are three main aeons of humanity. The original goddess-worshipping and nature-oriented Aeon of Isis includes most Stone Age civilizations and primitive goddess cults, and mainly represents a time in which humanity was beholden to the powers of the earth and female sexuality. It was characterized by a concern for the earthly over the heavenly, the feminine over the masculine, and the body over the mind. However, the goddess Isis eventually gave way to the god Osiris and his new aeon. Osiris is the "dying god" who experiences periodic cycles of death and rebirth. His era is oriented towards the heavens instead of the earth, and understands that it is the sun that is the true source of vitality and earthly life. Thus, the journey of resurrection takes center stage. The sun's symbolic "rebirth" after its three-day "death" during the winter Solstice was the magical formula of numerous Egyptian and Mithraic cults before being adopted as the central myth of Christianity. The Aeon of Osiris is thus characterized by a concern for the heavenly over the earthly, the masculine over the feminine, and the mind over the body.

By Crowley's time, however, this set of myths was waning in popularity. Due to humanity's more scientific mindset, people understood that the sun does not "die" every year. Rather, the Earth simply tilts on its axis, and the sun only *appears* to dim. Regardless of the season, the sun is still there in the vastness of space, as vibrant and luminous as ever. Pain, ignorance, and even death are likewise mere appearances; the shining star of the human spirit is always there to be realized. As the Book of the Law says, "Remember all ye that existence is pure joy; that all the sorrows are but as shadows; they pass and are done; but there is that which remains." As such, the new Aeon of Horus is not embodied by the mother or the father, but by their child, innocent, vital, and intelligent. This age, for Crowley, is characterized by a uniting of the feminine and masculine principles, and by a concern for individuality, love, and following one's own "True Will." In the Aeon of Horus, "Do what thou wilt shall be the whole of the Law."

For Crowley, this new law was the central concern driving his own Great Work. A prolific writer and performer, an impressive mythologist and ritualist, an early psychedelic pioneer, and an accomplished mountaineer, even Crowley's more earthly accomplishments are impressive. Though derided as a Satanist by culturally conservative early twentieth-century Britain (to be fair he did nothing to discourage this label), his primary aims were to bring about human freedom, enlightenment, love, and joy. To this end we the editors have selected several from amongst a vast body of works, which we feel embody his life's project and his unique style. From prophetic revelations to fictional accounts of drug-addled benders to practical instructions on ritual magic (and much in between), it is hard to deny that Crowley's works shine with the very charisma and originality that made him such an object of reverence and revulsion in the first place.

Rather than deride Crowley's as a philosophy of self-centeredness and/or decadence, as some insist, it is more helpful to understand his transformative effect on occult theory and practice. Indeed, Crowley's *Book of the Law* and its Aeon of Horus was revealed just prior to the wars of the early 20th century and the widespread disillusionment with rationality and institutions that followed shortly after. Crowley, in this way, may be the founder of post-modern magick. No longer beholden to tradition, religious authority, or even reason, many contemporary occultists now view magick as a personal creative act, a manifestation of the individual's "love under will" decoupled from the grand metaphysical systems used in centuries prior. Seen this way, Aleister Crowley's impact upon the occult tradition was nothing short of monumental. It would be difficult to argue that Crowley did not pave the way for the punk-post-modernist movement known as "Chaos Magick", an egalitarian, spontaneous, do-it-yourself approach to magick popularized in later in twentieth century, as well as for the contemporary neo-pagan, wiccan and shamanic teachings practiced by millions.

We do not put this collection forward in hopes of idealizing Crowley as an all-powerful magician or as the prophet of a new aeon. Indeed, "There is no great genius without some touch of madness." What we hope to to highlight here is a truly original and influential occult thinker whose writings pulse with vitality and relevance. Above all, we believe that Crowley continues to *matter*, especially in a society that seems intractably divided between a lifeless materialism and a rigid religious dogmatism. What Crowley offers is a way of living and thinking that is scientific and individualistic, but also mythic and metaphysical, that leaves room for both human intelligence and mystical inspiration. Hopefully it will become clear in the following pages that "Do What Thou Wilt," far from being a shallow hedonism, is an inexhaustibly complex moral and magical imperative. Crowley, though at various points considered a prophet, the Antichrist, an enlightened being, a miscreant obsessed with his celebrity, a powerful magician, and a dangerous cult leader, comes across to us as *real* and complex. In spite of, or more probably *because* of the many layers that call forth to us, what we find is an honest and original human being not afraid to let the old burn and build something newer and grander whose great shape we have likely only begun to fathom.

—Jake Dirnberger
Boulder, CO

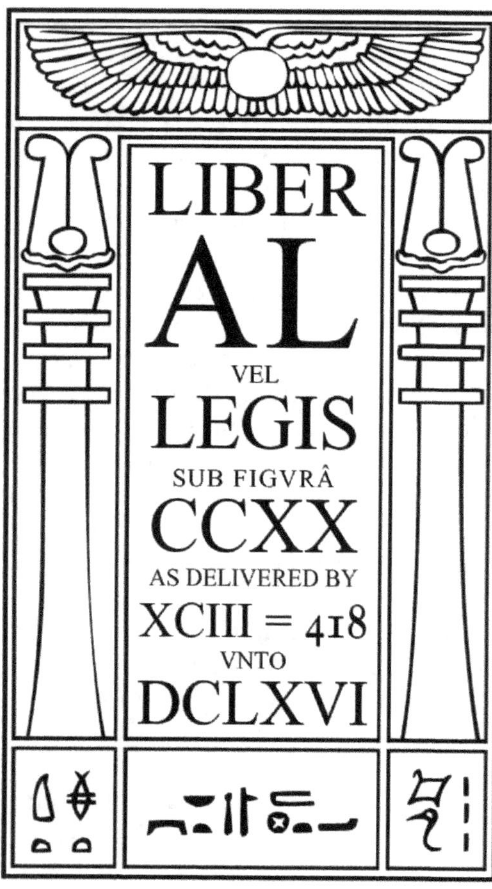
LIBER
AL
VEL
LEGIS
SUB FIGVRÂ
CCXX
AS DELIVERED BY
XCIII = 418
VNTO
DCLXVI

Introduction to the Book of the Law

I

The Book

1. This book was dictated in Cairo between noon and 1 p.m. on three successive days, April 8th, 9th, and 10th in the year 1904.

The Author called himself Aiwass, and claimed to be "the minister of Hoor-Paar-Kraat"; that is, a messenger from the forces ruling this earth at present, as will be explained later on.

How could he prove that he was in fact a being of a kind superior to any of the human race, and so entitled to speak with authority? Evidently he must show KNOWLEDGE and POWER such as no man has ever been known to possess.

2. He showed his KNOWLEDGE chiefly by the use of cipher or cryptogram in certain passages to set forth recondite facts, including some events which had yet to take place, such that no human being could possibly be aware of them; thus, the proof of his claim exists in the manuscript itself. It is independent of any human witness.

The study of these passages necessarily demands supreme human scholarship to interpret—it needs years of intense application. A great deal has still to be worked out. But enough has been discovered to justify his claim; the most sceptical intelligence is compelled to admit its truth.

This matter is best studied under the Master Therion, whose years of arduous research have led him to enlightenment.

On the other hand, the language of most of the Book is admirably simple, clear and vigorous. No one can read it without being stricken in the very core of his being.

3. The more than human POWER of Aiwass is shewn by the influence of his Master, and of the Book, upon actual

events: and history fully supports the claim made by him. These facts are appreciable by everyone; but are better understood with the help of the Master Therion.

4. The full detailed account of the events leading up to the dictation of this Book, with facsimile reproduction of the Manuscript and an essay by the Master Therion, is published in *The Equinox of the Gods*.

II
The Universe

This Book explains the Universe.

The elements are Nuit—Space—that is, the total of possibilities of every kind—and Hadit, any point which has experience of these possibilities. (This idea is for literary convenience symbolized by the Egyptian Goddess Nuit, a woman bending over like the Arch of the Night Sky. Hadit is symbolized as a Winged Globe at the heart of Nuit.)

Every event is a uniting of some one

monad with one of the experiences possible to it.

"Every man and every woman is a star," that is, an aggregate of such experiences, constantly changing with each fresh event, which affects him or her either consciously or subconsciously.

Each one of us has thus a universe of his own, but it is the same universe for each one as soon as it includes all possible experience. This implies the extension of consciousness to include all other consciousness.

In our present stage, the object that you see is never the same as the one that I see; we infer that it is the same because your experience tallies with mine on so many points that the actual differences of our observation are negligible. For instance, if a friend is walking between us, you see only his left side, I his right; but we agree that it is the same man, although we may differ not only as to what we may see of his body but as to what we know of his qualities. This conviction of identity grows stronger as we see him more often and get to know him better. Yet all the time neither of us can know anything of him at all beyond the total impression made on our respective minds.

The above is an extremely crude attempt to explain a system which reconciles all existing schools of philosophy.

III
The Law of Thelema[1]

This Book lays down a simple Code of Conduct.

"Do what thou wilt shall be the whole of the Law."

"Love is the law, love under will."

"There is no law beyond Do what thou wilt."

This means that each of us stars is to move on our true orbit, as marked out by the nature of our position, the law of our growth, the impulse of our past experiences. All events are equally lawful— and every one necessary, in the long run— for all

---

1. *Thelema is the Greek for Will, and has the same numerical value as Agape, the Greek for Love.*

of us, in theory; but in practice, only one act is lawful for each one of us at any given moment. Therefore Duty consists in determining to experience the right event from one moment of consciousness to another.

Each action or motion is an act of love, the uniting with one or another part of "Nuit"; each such act must be "under will," chosen so as to fulfil and not to thwart the true nature of the being concerned.

The technical methods of achieving this are to be studied in Magick, or acquired by personal instruction from the Master Therion and his appointed assistants.

IV
The New Aeon

The third chapter of the Book is difficult to understand, and may be very repugnant to many people born before the date of the book (April, 1904).

It tells us the characteristics of the Period on which we are now entered. Superficially, they appear appalling. We see some of them already with terrifying clarity. But fear not!

It explains that certain vast "stars" (or aggregates of experience) may be described as Gods. One of these is in charge of the destinies of this planet for periods of 2,000 years.[2] In the history of the world, as far as we know accurately, are three such Gods: Isis, the mother, when the Universe was conceived as simple nourishment drawn directly from her; this period is marked by matriarchal government.

Next, beginning 500 B.C., Osiris, the father, when the Universe was imagined as catastrophic, love, death, resurrection, as the method by which experience was built up; this corresponds to patriarchal systems.

Now, Horus, the child, in which we come to perceive events as a continual growth partaking in its elements of both these methods, and not to be overcome by circumstance. This present period involves the recognition of the individual as the unit of society.

---

2. *The moment of change from one period to another is technically called The Equinox of the Gods.*

We realize ourselves as explained in the first paragraphs of this essay. Every event, including death, is only one more accretion to our experience, freely willed by ourselves from the beginning and therefore also predestined.

This "God," Horus, has a technical title: Heru-Ra-Ha, a combination of twin gods, Ra-Hoor-Khuit and Hoor-Paar-Kraat. The meaning of this doctrine must be studied in *Magick*. (He is symbolized as a Hawk-Headed God enthroned.)

He rules the present period of 2,000 years, beginning in 1904. Everywhere his government is taking root. Observe for yourselves the decay of the sense of sin, the growth of innocence and irresponsibility, the strange modifications of the reproductive instinct with a tendency to become bisexual or epicene, the childlike confidence in progress combined with nightmare fear of catastrophe, against which we are yet half unwilling to take precautions.

Consider the outcrop of dictatorships, only possible when moral growth is in its earliest stages, and the prevalence of infantile cults like Communism, Fascism, Pacifism, Health Crazes, Occultism in nearly all its forms, religions sentimentalised to the point of practical extinction.

Consider the popularity of the cinema, the wireless, the football pools and guessing competitions, all devices for soothing fractious infants, no seed of purpose in them.

Consider sport, the babyish enthusiasms and rages which it excites, whole nations disturbed by disputes between boys.

Consider war, the atrocities which occur daily and leave us unmoved and hardly worried.

We are children.

How this new Aeon of Horus will develop, how the Child will grow up, these are for us to determine, growing up ourselves in the way of the Law of Thelema under the enlightened guidance of the Master Therion.

V
The Next Step

Democracy dodders.

Ferocious Fascism, cackling Communism, equally frauds, cavort crazily all over the globe.

They are hemming us in.

They are abortive births of the Child, the New Aeon of Horus.

Liberty stirs once more in the womb of Time.

Evolution makes its changes by anti-Socialistic ways. The "abnormal" man who foresees the trend of the times and adapts circumstance intelligently, is laughed at, persecuted, often destroyed by the herd; but he and his heirs, when the crisis comes, are survivors.

Above us today hangs a danger never yet paralleled in history. We suppress the individual in more and more ways. We think in terms of the herd. War no longer kills soldiers; it kills all indiscriminately. Every new measure of the most democratic and autocratic govenments is Communistic in essence. It is always restriction. We are all treated as imbecile children. Dora, the Shops Act, the Motoring Laws, Sunday suffocation, the Censorship—they won't trust us to cross the roads at will.

Fascism is like Communism, and dishonest into the bargain. The dictators suppress all art, literature, theatre, music, news, that does not meet their requirements; yet the world only moves by the light of genius. The herd will be destroyed in mass.

The establishment of the Law of Thelema is the only way to preserve individual liberty and to assure the future of the race.

In the words of the famous paradox of the Comte de Fénix—The absolute rule of the state shall be a function of the absolute liberty of each individual will.

All men and women are invited to cooperate with the Master Therion in this, the Great Work.

O. M.

Chapter I

1. Had! The manifestation of Nuit.

2. The unveiling of the company of heaven.

3. Every man and every woman is a star.

4. Every number is infinite; there is no difference.

5. Help me, o warrior lord of Thebes, in my unveiling before the Children of men!

6. Be thou Hadit, my secret centre, my heart & my tongue!

7. Behold! it is revealed by Aiwass the minister of Hoor-paar-kraat.

8. The Khabs is in the Khu, not the Khu in the Khabs.

9. Worship then the Khabs, and behold my light shed over you!

10. Let my servants be few & secret: they shall rule the many & the known.

11. These are fools that men adore; both their Gods & their men are fools.

12. Come forth, o children, under the stars, & take your fill of love!

13. I am above you and in you. My ecstasy is in yours. My joy is to see your joy.

14. Above, the gemmèd azure is
  The naked splendour of Nuit;
She bends in ecstasy to kiss
  The secret ardours of Hadit.
The wingèd globe, the starry blue,
  Are mine, O Ankh-af-na-khonsu!

15. Now ye shall know that the chosen priest & apostle of infinite space is the prince-priest the Beast; and in his woman called the Scarlet Woman is all power given. They shall gather my children into their fold: they shall bring the glory of the stars into the hearts of men.

16. For he is ever a sun, and she a moon. But to him is the winged secret flame, and to her the stooping starlight.

17. But ye are not so chosen.

18. Burn upon their brows, o splendrous serpent!

19. O azure-lidded woman, bend upon them!

20. The key of the rituals is in the secret word which I have given unto him.

21. With the God & the Adorer I am nothing: they do not see me. They are as upon the earth; I am Heaven, and there is no other God than me, and my lord Hadit.

22. Now, therefore, I am known to ye by my name Nuit, and to him by a secret name which I will give him when at last he knoweth me. Since I am Infinite Space, and the Infinite Stars thereof, do ye also

thus. Bind nothing! Let there be no difference made among you between any one thing & any other thing; for thereby there cometh hurt.

23. But whoso availeth in this, let him be the chief of all!

24. I am Nuit, and my word is six and fifty.

25. Divide, add, multiply, and understand.

26. Then saith the prophet and slave of the beauteous one: Who am I, and what shall be the sign? So she answered him, bending down, a lambent flame of blue, all-touching, all penetrant, her lovely hands upon the black earth, & her lithe body arched for love, and her soft feet not hurting the little flowers: Thou knowest! And the sign shall be my ecstasy, the consciousness of the continuity of existence, the omnipresence of my body.

27. Then the priest answered & said unto the Queen of Space, kissing her lovely

brows, and the dew of her light bathing his whole body in a sweet-smelling perfume of sweat: O Nuit, continuous one of Heaven, let it be ever thus; that men speak not of Thee as One but as None; and let them speak not of thee at all, since thou art continuous!

28. None, breathed the light, faint & faery, of the stars, and two.

29. For I am divided for love's sake, for the chance of union.

30. This is the creation of the world, that the pain of division is as nothing, and the joy of dissolution all.

31. For these fools of men and their woes care not thou at all! They feel little; what is, is balanced by weak joys; but ye are my chosen ones.

32. Obey my prophet! follow out the ordeals of my knowledge! seek me only! Then the joys of my love will redeem ye from all

pain. This is so: I swear it by the vault of my body; by my sacred heart and tongue; by all I can give, by all I desire of ye all.

33. Then the priest fell into a deep trance or swoon, & said unto the Queen of Heaven; Write unto us the ordeals; write unto us the rituals; write unto us the law!

34. But she said: the ordeals I write not: the rituals shall be half known and half concealed: the Law is for all.

35. This that thou writest is the threefold book of Law.

36. My scribe Ankh-af-na-khonsu, the priest of the princes, shall not in one letter change this book; but lest there be folly, he shall comment thereupon by the wisdom of Ra-Hoor-Khu-it.

37. Also the mantras and spells; the obeah and the wanga; the work of the wand and the work of the sword; these he shall learn and teach.

38. He must teach; but he may make severe the ordeals.

39. The word of the Law is Θελημα.

40. Who calls us Thelemites will do no wrong, if he look but close into the word. For there are therein Three Grades, the Hermit, and the Lover, and the man of Earth. Do what thou wilt shall be the whole of the Law.

41. The word of Sin is Restriction. O man! refuse not thy wife, if she will! O lover, if thou wilt, depart! There is no bond that can unite the divided but love: all else is a curse. Accurséd! Accurséd be it to the aeons! Hell.

42. Let it be that state of manyhood bound and loathing. So with thy all; thou hast no right but to do thy will.

43. Do that, and no other shall say nay.

44. For pure will, unassuaged of purpose,

delivered from the lust of result, is every way perfect.

45. The Perfect and the Perfect are one Perfect and not two; nay, are none!

46. Nothing is a secret key of this law. Sixty-one the Jews call it; I call it eight, eighty, four hundred & eighteen.

47. But they have the half: unite by thine art so that all disappear.

48. My prophet is a fool with his one, one, one; are not they the Ox, and none by the Book?

49. Abrogate are all rituals, all ordeals, all words and signs. Ra-Hoor-Khuit hath taken his seat in the East at the Equinox of the Gods; and let Asar be with Isa, who also are one. But they are not of me. Let Asar be the adorant, Isa the sufferer; Hoor in his secret name and splendour is the Lord initiating.

50. There is a word to say about the Hierophantic task. Behold! there are three ordeals in one, and it may be given in three ways. The gross must pass through fire; let the fine be tried in intellect, and the lofty chosen ones in the highest. Thus ye have star & star, system & system; let not one know well the other!

51. There are four gates to one palace; the floor of that palace is of silver and gold; lapis lazuli & jasper are there; and all rare scents; jasmine & rose, and the emblems of death. Let him enter in turn or at once the four gates; let him stand on the floor of the palace. Will he not sink? Amn. Ho! warrior, if thy servant sink? But there are means and means. Be goodly therefore: dress ye all in fine apparel; eat rich foods and drink sweet wines and wines that foam! Also, take your fill and will of love as ye will, when, where and with whom ye will! But always unto me.

52. If this be not aright; if ye confound the space-marks, saying: They are one; or saying, They are many; if the ritual be not ever

unto me: then expect the direful judgments of Ra Hoor Khuit!

53. This shall regenerate the world, the little world my sister, my heart & my tongue, unto whom I send this kiss. Also, o scribe and prophet, though thou be of the princes, it shall not assuage thee nor absolve thee. But ecstasy be thine and joy of earth: ever To me! To me!

54. Change not as much as the style of a letter; for behold! thou, o prophet, shalt not behold all these mysteries hidden therein.

55. The child of thy bowels, he shall behold them.

56. Expect him not from the East, nor from the West; for from no expected house cometh that child. Aum! All words are sacred and all prophets true; save only that they understand a little; solve the first half of the equation, leave the second unattacked. But thou hast all in the clear light, and some, though not all, in the dark.

57. Invoke me under my stars! Love is the law, love under will. Nor let the fools mistake love; for there are love and love. There is the dove, and there is the serpent. Choose ye well! He, my prophet, hath chosen, knowing the law of the fortress, and the great mystery of the House of God.

All these old letters of my Book are aright; but צ is not the Star. This also is secret: my prophet shall reveal it to the wise.

58. I give unimaginable joys on earth: certainty, not faith, while in life, upon death; peace unutterable, rest, ecstasy; nor do I demand aught in sacrifice.

59. My incense is of resinous woods & gums; and there is no blood therein: because of my hair the trees of Eternity.

60. My number is 11, as all their numbers who are of us. The Five Pointed Star, with a Circle in the Middle, & the circle is Red. My colour is black to the blind, but the blue & gold are seen of the seeing. Also I have a secret glory for them that love me.

61. But to love me is better than all things: if under the night-stars in the desert thou presently burnest mine incense before me, invoking me with a pure heart, and the Serpent flame therein, thou shalt come a little to lie in my bosom. For one kiss wilt thou then be willing to give all; but whoso gives one particle of dust shall lose all in that hour. Ye shall gather goods and store of women and spices; ye shall wear rich jewels; ye shall exceed the nations of the earth in splendour & pride; but always in the love of me, and so shall ye come to my joy. I charge you earnestly to come before me in a single robe, and covered with a rich headdress. I love you! I yearn to you! Pale or purple, veiled or voluptuous, I who am all pleasure and purple, and drunkenness of the innermost sense, desire you. Put on the wings, and arouse the coiled splendour within you: come unto me!

62. At all my meetings with you shall the priestess say— and her eyes shall burn with desire as she stands bare and rejoicing in my secret temple— To me! To me! calling

forth the flame of the hearts of all in her love-chant.

63. Sing the rapturous love-song unto me! Burn to me perfumes! Wear to me jewels! Drink to me, for I love you! I love you!

64. I am the blue-lidded daughter of Sunset; I am the naked brilliance of the voluptuous night-sky.

65. To me! To me!

66. The Manifestation of Nuit is at an end.

Chapter II

1. Nu! the hiding of Hadit.

2. Come! all ye, and learn the secret that hath not yet been revealed. I, Hadit, am the complement of Nu, my bride. I am not extended, and Khabs is the name of my House.

3. In the sphere I am everywhere the centre, as she, the circumference, is nowhere found.

4. Yet she shall be known & I never.

5. Behold! the rituals of the old time are black. Let the evil ones be cast away; let the good ones be purged by the prophet! Then shall this Knowledge go aright.

6. I am the flame that burns in every heart of man, and in the core of every star. I am Life, and the giver of Life, yet therefore is the knowledge of me the knowledge of death.

7. I am the Magician and the Exorcist. I am the axle of the wheel, and the cube in the circle. "Come unto me" is a foolish word: for it is I that go.

8. Who worshipped Heru-pa-kraath have worshipped me; ill, for I am the worshipper.

9. Remember all ye that existence is pure joy; that all the sorrows are but as shadows; they pass & are done; but there is that which remains.

10. O prophet! thou hast ill will to learn this writing.

11. I see thee hate the hand & the pen; but I am stronger.

12. Because of me in Thee which thou knewest not.

13. for why? Because thou wast the knower, and me.

14. Now let there be a veiling of this shrine: now let the light devour men and eat them up with blindness!

15. For I am perfect, being Not; and my number is nine by the fools; but with the just I am eight, and one in eight: Which is vital, for I am none indeed. The Empress

and the King are not of me; for there is a further secret.

16. I am The Empress & the Hierophant. Thus eleven, as my bride is eleven.

17. Hear me, ye people of sighing!
  The sorrows of pain and regret
Are left to the dead and the dying,
  The folk that not know me as yet.

18. These are dead, these fellows; they feel not. We are not for the poor and sad: the lords of the earth are our kinsfolk.

19. Is a God to live in a dog? No! but the highest are of us. They shall rejoice, our chosen: who sorroweth is not of us.

20. Beauty and strength, leaping laughter and delicious languor, force and fire, are of us.

21. We have nothing with the outcast and the unfit: let them die in their misery. For they feel not. Compassion is the vice of

kings: stamp down the wretched & the weak: this is the law of the strong: this is our law and the joy of the world. Think not, o king, upon that lie: That Thou Must Die: verily thou shalt not die, but live. Now let it be understood: If the body of the King dissolve, he shall remain in pure ecstasy for ever. Nuit! Hadit! Ra-Hoor-Khuit! The Sun, Strength & Sight, Light; these are for the servants of the Star & the Snake.

22. I am the Snake that giveth Knowledge & Delight and bright glory, and stir the hearts of men with drunkenness. To worship me take wine and strange drugs whereof I will tell my prophet, & be drunk thereof! They shall not harm ye at all. It is a lie, this folly against self. The exposure of innocence is a lie. Be strong, o man! lust, enjoy all things of sense and rapture: fear not that any God shall deny thee for this.

23. I am alone: there is no God where I am.

24. Behold! these be grave mysteries; for there are also of my friends who be hermits.

Now think not to find them in the forest or on the mountain; but in beds of purple, caressed by magnificent beasts of women with large limbs, and fire and light in their eyes, and masses of flaming hair about them; there shall ye find them. Ye shall see them at rule, at victorious armies, at all the joy; and there shall be in them a joy a million times greater than this. Beware lest any force another, King against King! Love one another with burning hearts; on the low men trample in the fierce lust of your pride, in the day of your wrath.

25. Ye are against the people, O my chosen!

26. I am the secret Serpent coiled about to spring: in my coiling there is joy. If I lift up my head, I and my Nuit are one. If I droop down mine head, and shoot forth venom, then is rapture of the earth, and I and the earth are one.

27. There is great danger in me; for who doth not understand these runes shall make a great miss. He shall fall down into

the pit called Because, and there he shall perish with the dogs of Reason.

28. Now a curse upon Because and his kin!

29. May Because be accursèd for ever!

30. If Will stops and cries Why, invoking Because, then Will stops & does nought.

31. If Power asks why, then is Power weakness.

32. Also reason is a lie; for there is a factor infinite & unknown; & all their words are skew-wise.

33. Enough of Because! Be he damned for a dog!

34. But ye, o my people, rise up & awake!

35. Let the rituals be rightly performed with joy & beauty!

36. There are rituals of the elements and feasts of the times.

37. A feast for the first night of the Prophet and his Bride!

38. A feast for the three days of the writing of the Book of the Law.

39. A feast for Tahuti and the child of the Prophet— secret, O Prophet!

40. A feast for the Supreme Ritual, and a feast for the Equinox of the Gods.

41. A feast for fire and a feast for water; a feast for life and a greater feast for death!

42. A feast every day in your hearts in the joy of my rapture!

43. A feast every night unto Nu, and the pleasure of uttermost delight!

44. Aye! feast! rejoice! there is no dread hereafter. There is the dissolution, and

eternal ecstasy in the kisses of Nu.

45. There is death for the dogs.

46. Dost thou fail? Art thou sorry? Is fear in thine heart?

47. Where I am these are not.

48. Pity not the fallen! I never knew them. I am not for them. I console not: I hate the consoled & the consoler.

49. I am unique & conqueror. I am not of the slaves that perish. Be they damned & dead! Amen. (This is of the 4: there is a fifth who is invisible, & therein am I as a babe in an egg.)

50. Blue am I and gold in the light of my bride: but the red gleam is in my eyes; & my spangles are purple & green.

51. Purple beyond purple: it is the light higher than eyesight.

52. There is a veil: that veil is black. It is the veil of the modest woman; it is the veil of sorrow, & the pall of death: this is none of me. Tear down that lying spectre of the centuries: veil not your vices in virtuous words: these vices are my service; ye do well, & I will reward you here and hereafter.

53. Fear not, o prophet, when these words are said, thou shalt not be sorry. Thou art emphatically my chosen; and blessed are the eyes that thou shalt look upon with gladness. But I will hide thee in a mask of sorrow: they that see thee shall fear thou art fallen: but I lift thee up.

54. Nor shall they who cry aloud their folly that thou meanest nought avail; thou shall reveal it: thou availest: they are the slaves of because: They are not of me. The stops as thou wilt; the letters? change them not in style or value!

55. Thou shalt obtain the order & value of the English Alphabet; thou shalt find new

symbols to attribute them unto.

56. Begone! ye mockers; even though ye laugh in my honour ye shall laugh not long: then when ye are sad know that I have forsaken you.

57. He that is righteous shall be righteous still; he that is filthy shall be filthy still.

58. Yea! deem not of change: ye shall be as ye are, & not other. Therefore the kings of the earth shall be Kings for ever: the slaves shall serve. There is none that shall be cast down or lifted up: all is ever as it was. Yet there are masked ones my servants: it may be that yonder beggar is a King. A King may choose his garment as he will: there is no certain test: but a beggar cannot hide his poverty.

59. Beware therefore! Love all, lest perchance is a King concealed! Say you so? Fool! If he be a King, thou canst not hurt him.

60. Therefore strike hard & low, and to hell with them, master!

61. There is a light before thine eyes, o prophet, a light undesired, most desirable.

62. I am uplifted in thine heart; and the kisses of the stars rain hard upon thy body.

63. Thou art exhaust in the voluptuous fullness of the inspiration; the expiration is sweeter than death, more rapid and laughterful than a caress of Hell's own worm.

64. Oh! thou art overcome: we are upon thee; our delight is all over thee: hail! hail: prophet of Nu! prophet of Had! prophet of Ra-Hoor-Khu! Now rejoice! now come in our splendour & rapture! Come in our passionate peace, & write sweet words for the Kings!

65. I am the Master: thou art the Holy Chosen One.

66. Write, & find ecstasy in writing! Work,

& be our bed in working! Thrill with the joy of life & death! Ah! thy death shall be lovely: whoso seeth it shall be glad. Thy death shall be the seal of the promise of our agelong love. Come! lift up thine heart & rejoice! We are one; we are none.

67. Hold! Hold! Bear up in thy rapture; fall not in swoon of the excellent kisses!

68. Harder! Hold up thyself! Lift thine head! breathe not so deep— die!

69. Ah! Ah! What do I feel? Is the word exhausted?

70. There is help & hope in other spells. Wisdom says: be strong! Then canst thou bear more joy. Be not animal; refine thy rapture! If thou drink, drink by the eight and ninety rules of art: if thou love, exceed by delicacy; and if thou do aught joyous, let there be subtlety therein!

71. But exceed! exceed!

72. Strive ever to more! and if thou art truly mine— and doubt it not, an if thou art ever joyous!— death is the crown of all.

73. Ah! Ah! Death! Death! thou shalt long for death. Death is forbidden, o man, unto thee.

74. The length of thy longing shall be the strength of its glory. He that lives long & desires death much is ever the King among the Kings.

75. Aye! listen to the numbers & the words:

76. 4 6 3 8 A B K 2 4 A L G M O R 3 Y X 24 89 R P S T O V A L. What meaneth this, o prophet? Thou knowest not; nor shalt thou know ever. There cometh one to follow thee: he shall expound it. But remember, o chosen one, to be me; to follow the love of Nu in the star-lit heaven; to look forth upon men, to tell them this glad word.

77. O be thou proud and mighty among men!

78. Lift up thyself! for there is none like unto thee among men or among Gods! Lift up thyself, o my prophet, thy stature shall surpass the stars. They shall worship thy name, foursquare, mystic, wonderful, the number of the man; and the name of thy house 418.

79. The end of the hiding of Hadit; and blessing & worship to the prophet of the lovely Star!

Chapter III

1. Abrahadabra; the reward of Ra Hoor Khut.

2. There is division hither homeward; there is a word not known. Spelling is defunct; all is not aught. Beware! Hold! Raise the spell of Ra-Hoor-Khuit!

3. Now let it be first understood that I am a god of War and of Vengeance. I shall deal hardly with them.

4. Choose ye an island!

5. Fortify it!

6. Dung it about with enginery of war!

7. I will give you a war-engine.

8. With it ye shall smite the peoples; and none shall stand before you.

9. Lurk! Withdraw! Upon them! this is the Law of the Battle of Conquest: thus shall my worship be about my secret house.

10. Get the stélé of revealing itself; set it in thy secret temple— and that temple is already aright disposed— & it shall be your Kiblah for ever. It shall not fade, but miraculous colour shall come back to it day after day. Close it in locked glass for a proof to the world.

11. This shall be your only proof. I forbid argument. Conquer! That is enough. I will

make easy to you the abstruction from the ill-ordered house in the Victorious City. Thou shalt thyself convey it with worship, o prophet, though thou likest it not. Thou shalt have danger & trouble. Ra-Hoor-Khu is with thee. Worship me with fire & blood; worship me with swords & with spears. Let the woman be girt with a sword before me: let blood flow to my name. Trample down the Heathen; be upon them, o warrior, I will give you of their flesh to eat!

12. Sacrifice cattle, little and big: after a child.

13. But not now.

14. Ye shall see that hour, o blessèd Beast, and thou the Scarlet Concubine of his desire!

15. Ye shall be sad thereof.

16. Deem not too eagerly to catch the promises; fear not to undergo the curses. Ye, even ye, know not this meaning all.

17. Fear not at all; fear neither men nor Fates, nor gods, nor anything. Money fear not, nor laughter of the folk folly, nor any other power in heaven or upon the earth or under the earth. Nu is your refuge as Hadit your light; and I am the strength, force, vigour, of your arms.

18. Mercy let be off: damn them who pity! Kill and torture; spare not; be upon them!

19. That stélé they shall call the Abomination of Desolation; count well its name, & it shall be to you as 718.

20. Why? Because of the fall of Because, that he is not there again.

21. Set up my image in the East: thou shalt buy thee an image which I will show thee, especial, not unlike the one thou knowest. And it shall be suddenly easy for thee to do this.

22. The other images group around me to support me: let all be worshipped, for they

shall cluster to exalt me. I am the visible object of worship; the others are secret; for the Beast & his Bride are they: and for the winners of the Ordeal x. What is this? Thou shalt know.

23. For perfume mix meal & honey & thick leavings of red wine: then oil of Abramelin and olive oil, and afterward soften & smooth down with rich fresh blood.

24. The best blood is of the moon, monthly: then the fresh blood of a child, or dropping from the host of heaven: then of enemies; then of the priest or of the worshippers: last of some beast, no matter what.

25. This burn: of this make cakes & eat unto me. This hath also another use; let it be laid before me, and kept thick with perfumes of your orison: it shall become full of beetles as it were and creeping things sacred unto me.

26. These slay, naming your enemies; & they shall fall before you.

27. Also these shall breed lust & power of lust in you at the eating thereof.

28. Also ye shall be strong in war.

29. Moreover, be they long kept, it is better; for they swell with my force. All before me.

30. My altar is of open brass work: burn thereon in silver or gold!

31. There cometh a rich man from the West who shall pour his gold upon thee.

32. From gold forge steel!

33. Be ready to fly or to smite!

34. But your holy place shall be untouched throughout the centuries: though with fire and sword it be burnt down & shattered, yet an invisible house there standeth, and shall stand until the fall of the Great Equinox; when Hrumachis shall arise and the double-wanded one assume my throne and

place. Another prophet shall arise, and bring fresh fever from the skies; another woman shall awake the lust & worship of the Snake; another soul of God and beast shall mingle in the globèd priest; another sacrifice shall stain the tomb; another king shall reign; and blessing no longer be poured To the Hawk-headed mystical Lord!

35. The half of the word of Heru-ra-ha, called Hoor-pa-kraat and Ra-Hoor-Khut.

36. Then said the prophet unto the God:

37. I adore thee in the song:—

I am the Lord of Thebes, and I
  The inspired forth-speaker of Mentu;
For me unveils the veilèd sky,
  The self-slain Ankh-af-na-khonsu
Whose words are truth. I invoke, I greet
  Thy presence, O Ra-Hoor-Khuit!
Unity uttermost showed!
  I adore the might of Thy breath,
Supreme and terrible God,
  Who makest the gods and death

To tremble before Thee—
    I, I adore thee!
Appear on the throne of Ra!
    Open the ways of the Khu!
Lighten the ways of the Ka!
    The ways of the Khabs run through
To stir me or still me!
    Aum! let it kill me!

38. So that thy light is in me; & its red flame is as a sword in my hand to push thy order. There is a secret door that I shall make to establish thy way in all the quarters, (these are the adorations, as thou hast written), as it is said:

The light is mine; its rays consume
    Me: I have made a secret door
Into the House of Ra and Tum,
    Of Khephra and of Ahathoor.
I am thy Theban, O Mentu,
    The prophet Ankh-af-na-khonsu!
By Bes-na-Maut my breast I beat;
    By wise Ta-Nech I weave my spell.
Show thy star-splendour, O Nuit!
    Bid me within thine House to dwell,

O wingèd snake of light, Hadit!
Abide with me, Ra-Hoor-Khuit!

39. All this and a book to say how thou didst come hither and a reproduction of this ink and paper for ever— for in it is the word secret & not only in the English— and thy comment upon this the Book of the Law shall be printed beautifully in red ink and black upon beautiful paper made by hand; and to each man and woman that thou meetest, were it but to dine or to drink at them, it is the Law to give. Then they shall chance to abide in this bliss or no; it is no odds. Do this quickly!

40. But the work of the comment? That is easy; and Hadit burning in thy heart shall make swift and secure thy pen.

41. Establish at thy Kaaba a clerk-house: all must be done well and with business way.

42. The ordeals thou shalt oversee thyself, save only the blind ones. Refuse none, but thou shalt know & destroy the traitors. I

am Ra-Hoor-Khuit; and I am powerful to protect my servant. Success is thy proof: argue not; convert not; talk not overmuch! Them that seek to entrap thee, to overthrow thee, them attack without pity or quarter; & destroy them utterly. Swift as a trodden serpent turn and strike! Be thou yet deadlier than he! Drag down their souls to awful torment: laugh at their fear: spit upon them!

43. Let the Scarlet Woman beware! If pity and compassion and tenderness visit her heart; if she leave my work to toy with old sweetnesses; then shall my vengeance be known. I will slay me her child: I will alienate her heart: I will cast her out from men: as a shrinking and despised harlot shall she crawl through dusk wet streets, and die cold and an-hungered.

44. But let her raise herself in pride! Let her follow me in my way! Let her work the work of wickedness! Let her kill her heart! Let her be loud and adulterous! Let her be

covered with jewels, and rich garments, and let her be shameless before all men!

45. Then will I lift her to pinnacles of power: then will I breed from her a child mightier than all the kings of the earth. I will fill her with joy: with my force shall she see & strike at the worship of Nu: she shall achieve Hadit.

46. I am the warrior Lord of the Forties: the Eighties cower before me, & are abased. I will bring you to victory & joy: I will be at your arms in battle & ye shall delight to slay. Success is your proof; courage is your armour; go on, go on, in my strength; & ye shall turn not back for any!

47. This book shall be translated into all tongues: but always with the original in the writing of the Beast; for in the chance shape of the letters and their position to one another: in these are mysteries that no Beast shall divine. Let him not seek to try: but one cometh after him, whence I say not, who shall discover the Key of it all.

Then this line drawn is a key: then this circle squared in its failure is a key also. And Abrahadabra. It shall be his child & that strangely. Let him not seek after this; for thereby alone can he fall from it.

48. Now this mystery of the letters is done, and I want to go on to the holier place.

49. I am in a secret fourfold word, the blasphemy against all gods of men.

50. Curse them! Curse them! Curse them!

51. With my Hawk's head I peck at the eyes of Jesus as he hangs upon the cross.

52. I flap my wings in the face of Mohammed & blind him.

53. With my claws I tear out the flesh of the Indian and the Buddhist, Mongol and Din.

54. Bahlasti! Ompehda! I spit on your crapulous creeds.

55. Let Mary inviolate be torn upon wheels: for her sake let all chaste women be utterly despised among you!

56. Also for beauty's sake and love's!

57. Despise also all cowards; professional soldiers who dare not fight, but play; all fools despise!

58. But the keen and the proud, the royal and the lofty; ye are brothers!

59. As brothers fight ye!

60. There is no law beyond Do what thou wilt.

61. There is an end of the word of the God enthroned in Ra's seat, lightening the girders of the soul.

62. To Me do ye reverence! to me come ye through tribulation of ordeal, which is bliss.

63. The fool readeth this Book of the Law, and its comment; & he understandeth it not.

64. Let him come through the first ordeal, & it will be to him as silver.

65. Through the second, gold.

66. Through the third, stones of precious water.

67. Through the fourth, ultimate sparks of the intimate fire.

68. Yet to all it shall seem beautiful. Its enemies who say not so, are mere liars.

69. There is success.

70. I am the Hawk-Headed Lord of Silence & of Strength; my nemyss shrouds the night-blue sky.

71. Hail! ye twin warriors about the pillars of the world! for your time is nigh at hand.

72. I am the Lord of the Double Wand of Power; the wand of the Force of Coph Nia— but my left hand is empty, for I have crushed an Universe; & nought remains.

73. Paste the sheets from right to left and from top to bottom: then behold!

74. There is a splendour in my name hidden and glorious, as the sun of midnight is ever the son.

75. The ending of the words is the Word Abrahadabra.

The Book of the Law is Written
and Concealed.
Aum. Ha.

The Comment

Do what thou wilt shall be the whole of the Law.

The study of this Book is forbidden. It is wise to destroy this copy after the first reading.

Whosoever disregards this does so at his own risk and peril. These are most dire.

Those who discuss the contents of this Book are to be shunned by all, as centres of pestilence.

All questions of the Law are to be decided only by appeal to my writings, each for himself.

There is no law beyond Do what thou wilt.

Love is the law, love under will.

The priest of the princes,
ANKH-F-N-KHONSU

ΚΕΦΑΛΗ Β
The Cry of the Hawk

Hoor hath a secret fourfold name; it is Do What Thou Wilt[1].

Four words: Naught—One—Many—All.

Thou—Child!

Thy Name is holy.

Thy Kingdom is come.

Thy Will is done.

Here is the Bread.

Here is the Blood.

Bring us through Temptation!

1. *Fourteen letters. Quid Voles Illud Fac. Q.V.I.F. 196 = 142.*

Deliver us from Good and Evil!

That Mine as Thine be the Crown of the Kingdom, even now.

ABRAHADABRA.

These ten words are four, the Name of the One.

COMMENTARY (B)

The "Hawk" referred to is Horus.

The chapter begins with a comment on Liber Legis III, 49.

Those four words, Do What Thou Wilt, are also identified with the four possible modes of conceiving the universe; Horus unites these.

Follows a version of the "Lord's Prayer", suitable to Horus... There are ten sections in this prayer, and, as the prayer is attributed to Horus, they are called four, as above explained; but it is only the name of Horus which is fourfold; He himself is one.

This may be compared with the Qabalistic doctrine of the Ten Sephiroth as an expression of Tetragrammaton (1 plus 2 plus 3 plus 4 = 10).

It is now seen that this Hawk is not Solar, but Mercurial; hence the words, the Cry of the Hawk, the essential part of Mercury being his Voice; and the number of the chapter, B, which is Beth the letter of Mercury, the Magus of the Tarot, who has four weapons, and it must be remembered that this card is numbered 1, again connecting all these symbols with the Phallus.

The essential weapon of Mercury is the Caduceus.

Absinthe: The Green Goddess

I.

Keep always this dim corner for me, that I may sit while the Green Hour glides, a proud pavine of Time. For I am no longer in the city accursed, where Time is horsed on the white gelding Death, his spurs rusted with blood.

There is a corner of the United States which he has overlooked. It lies in New Orleans, between Canal Street and Esplanade Avenue; the Mississippi for its base. Thence it reaches northward to a most curious desert land, where is a cemetery lovely beyond dreams. Its walls low and whitewashed, within which straggles a wilderness of strange and fantastic tombs; and hard by is that great city of brothels which is so cynically mirthful a neighbor. As Felicien Rops wrote— or was it Edmond d'Haraucourt?— "*la Prostitution et la Mort sont frere et soeur— les fils de Dieu!*" At least the poet of *Le Legende des Sexes* was right, and the psycho-analysts after him, in identifying the Mother with the Tomb. This, then, is only the beginning and end of things, this "quartier macabre" beyond the North Rampart with the Mississippi on the other side. It is like the space between, our life which flows, and fertilizes as it flows, muddy and malarious as it may be, to empty itself into the warm bosom of the Gulf Stream, which (in our allegory) we may call the Life of God.

But our business is with the heart of things; we must go beyond the crude phenomena of nature if we are to dwell in the spirit. Art is the soul of life and the Old Absinthe House is heart and soul of the old quarter of New Orleans.

For here was the headquarters of no common man— no less than a real pirate— of Captain Lafitte, who not only robbed his neighbors, but defended them against invasion. Here, too, sat Henry Clay, who lived and died to give his name to a cigar.

Outside this house no man remembers much more of him than that; but here, authentic and, as I imagine, indignant, his ghost stalks grimly.

Here, too are marble basins hollowed— and hallowed! — by the drippings of the water which creates by baptism the new spirit of absinthe.

I am only sipping the second glass of that "fascinating, but subtle poison, whose ravages eat men's heart and brain" that I have ever tasted in my life; and as I am not an American anxious for quick action, I am not surprised and disappointed that I do not drop dead upon the spot. But I can taste souls without the aid of absinthe; and besides, this is magic of absinthe! The spirit of the house has entered into it; it is an elixir, the masterpiece of an old alchemist, no common wine.

And so, as I talk with the patron concerning the vanity of things, I perceive the secret of the heart of God himself; this, that everything, even the vilest thing, is so unutterably lovely that it is worthy of the devotion of a God for all eternity.

What other excuse could He give man for making him? In substance, that is my answer to King Solomon.

II.

The barrier between divine and human things is frail but inviolable; the artist and the bourgeois are only divided by a point of view — "A hair divided the false and true."

I am watching the opalescence of my absinthe, and it leads me to ponder upon a certain very curious mystery, persistent in legend. We may call it the mystery of the rainbow.

Originally in the fantastic but significant legend of the Hebrews, the rainbow is mentioned as the sign of salvation. The world has been purified by water, and was ready for the revelation of Wine. God would never again destroy His work, but ultimately seal its perfection by a baptism of fire.

Now, in this analogue also falls the coat of many colors which was made for Joseph, a legend which was regarded as so important that it was subsequently borrowed for the romance of Jesus. The veil of the Temple, too, was of many colors. We find, further east, that the Manipura Cakkra—the Lotus of the City of Jewels—which is an important center in Hindu anatomy, and apparently identical with the solar plexus, is the central point of the nervous system of the human body, dividing the sacred from the profane, or the lower from the higher.

In western Mysticism, once more we learn that the middle grade initiation is called Hodos Camelioniis, the Path of the Chameleon. There is here evidently an illusion to this same mystery. We also learn that the middle stage in Alchemy is when the liquor becomes opalescent.

Finally, we note among the visions of the Saints one called the Universal Peacock, in which the totality is perceived thus royally appareled.

Would it were possible to assemble in this place the cohorts of quotation; for indeed they are beautiful with banners, flashing their myriad rays from cothurn and habergeon, gay and gallant in the light of that Sun which knows no fall from Zenith of high noon!

Yet I must needs already have written so much to make clear one pitiful conceit: can it be that in the opalescence of absinthe is some occult link with this mystery of the Rainbow? For undoubtedly one does indefinably and subtly insinuate the drinker in the secret chamber of Beauty, does kindle his thoughts to rapture, adjust his point of view to that of the artists, at least to that degree of which he is originally capable, weave for his fancy a gala dress of stuff as many-colored as the mind of Aphrodite.

Oh Beauty! Long did I love thee, long did I pursue thee, thee elusive, thee intangible! And lo! thou enfoldest me by night and day in the arms of gracious, of luxurious, of shimmering silence.

III.

The Prohibitionist must always be a person of no moral character; for he cannot even conceive of the possibility of a man capable of resisting temptation. Still more, he is so obsessed, like the savage, by the fear of the unknown, that he regards alcohol as a fetish, necessarily alluring and tyrannical.

With this ignorance of human nature goes an ever grosser ignorance of the divine nature. He does not understand that the universe has only one possible purpose; that, the business of life being happily completed by the production of the necessities and luxuries incidental to comfort, the residuum of human energy needs an outlet. The surplus of Will must find issue in the elevation of the individual towards the Godhead; and the method of such elevation is by religion, love, and art. These three things are indissolubly bound up with wine, for they are species of intoxication.

Yet against all these things we find the prohibitionist, logically enough. It is true that he usually pretends to admit religion as a proper pursuit for humanity; but what a religion! He has removed from it every element of ecstasy or even of devotion; in his hands it has become cold, fanatical, cruel, and stupid, a thing merciless and formal, without sympathy or humanity. Love and art he rejects altogether; for him the only meaning of love is a mechanical—hardly even physiological!—process necessary for the perpetuation of the human race. (But why perpetuate it?) Art is for him the parasite and pimp of love. He cannot distinguish between the Apollo Belvedere and the crude bestialities of certain Pompeian frescoes, or between Rabelais and Elenor Glyn.

What then is his ideal of human life? One cannot say. So crass a creature can have no true ideal. There have been ascetic philosophers; but the prohibitionist would be as offended by their doctrine as by ours, which, indeed, are not so dissimilar as appears. Wage-slavery and boredom seem to complete his outlook on the world. There are species which survive because of the feeling of disgust inspired by them: one is reluctant to set the heel firmly upon them, however thick may be one's boots. But when they are recognized as utterly noxious to humanity—the more so that they ape its form—then courage must be found, or, rather, nausea must be swallowed. May God send us a Saint George!

IV.

It is notorious that all genius is accompanied by vice. Almost always this takes the form of sexual extravagance. It is to be observed that deficiency, as in the cases of Carlyle and Ruskin, is to be reckoned as extravagance. At least the word abnormalcy will fit all cases. Farther, we see that in a very large number of great men there has also been indulgence in drink or drugs. There are whole periods when practically every great man has been thus marked, and these periods are those during which the heroic spirit has died out of their nation, and the bourgeois is apparently triumphant.

In this case the cause is evidently the horror of life induced in the artist by the contemplation of his surroundings. He must find another world, no matter at what cost. Consider the end of the eighteenth century. In France, the men of genius are made, so to speak, possible, by the Revolution. In England, under Castlereagh, we find Blake lost to humanity in mysticism, Shelley and Byron exiles, Coleridge taking refuge in opium, Keats sinking under the weight of circumstance, Wordsworth forced to sell his soul, while the enemy, in the persons of Southey and Moore, triumphantly holds sway.

The poetically similar period in France is 1850 to 1870. Hugo is in exile, and all his brethren are given to absinthe or to hashish or to opium.

There is however another consideration more important. There are some men who possess the understanding of the City of God, and know not the keys; or, if they possess them, have not force to turn them in the wards. Such men often seek to win heaven by forged credentials. Just so a youth who desires love is too often deceived by simulacra, embraces Lydia, thinking her to be Lalage.

But the greatest men of all suffer neither the limitations of the former class nor the illusions of the latter. Yet we find them equally given to what is apparently indulgence. Lombroso has foolishly sought to find the source of this in madness—as if insanity could scale the peaks of Progress while Reason recoiled from the bergschrund. The explanation is far otherwise. Imagine to yourself the mental state of him who inherits or attains the full consciousness of the artist, that is to say, the divine consciousness.

He finds himself unutterably lonely, and he must steel himself to endure it. All his peers are dead long since! Even if he find an equal upon earth, there can scarcely be companionship, hardly more than the far courtesy of king to king. There are no twin souls in genius.

Good—he can reconcile himself to the scorn of the world. But yet he feels with anguish his duty towards it. It is therefore essential to him to be human.

Now the divine consciousness is not full flowered in youth. The newness of the objective world preoccupies the soul for many years. It is only as each illusion vanishes before the magic of the master that he gains more and more the power to dwell in the world of Reality. And with this comes the terrible temptation—the desire to enter and enjoy rather than remain among men and suffer their illusions. Yet, since the sole purpose of the incarnation of such a Master was to help humanity, they must make the supreme renunciation. It is the problem of the dreadful bridge of Islam, Al Sirak—the razor-edge will cut the unwary foot, yet it must be trodden firmly, or the traveler will fall to the abyss. I dare not sit in the Old Absinthe House forever, wrapped in the ineffable delight of the Beatific Vision. I must write this essay, that men may thereby come at last to understand true things. But the operation of the creative godhead is not enough. Art is itself too near the reality which must be renounced for a season.

Therefore his work is also part of his temptation; the genius feels himself slipping constantly heavenward. The gravitation of eternity draws him. He is like a ship torn by the tempest from the harbor where the master must needs take on new passengers to the Happy Isles. So he must throw out anchors and the only holding is the mire! Thus in order to maintain the equilibrium of sanity, the artist is obliged to seek fellowship with the grossest of mankind. Like Lord Dunsany or Augustus John, today, or like Teniers or old, he may love to sit in taverns where sailors frequent; or he may wander the country with Gypsies, or he may form liaisons with the vilest men and women. Edward Fitzgerald would see an illiterate fisherman and spend weeks in his company. Verlaine made associates of Rimbaud and Bibi la Puree. Shakespeare consorted with the Earls of Pembroke and Southampton. Marlowe was actually killed during a brawl in a low tavern. And when we consider the sex-relation, it is hard to mention a genius who had a wife or mistress of even tolerable good character. If he had one, he would be sure to neglect her for a Vampire or a Shrew. A good woman is too near that heaven of Reality which he is sworn to renounce!

And this, I suppose, is why I am interested in the woman who has come to sit at the nearest table. Let us find out her story; let us try to see with the eyes of her soul!

V.

She is a woman of no more than thirty years of age, though she looks older. She comes here at irregular intervals, once a week or once a month, but when she comes she sits down to get solidly drunk on that alternation of beer and gin which the best authorities in England deem so efficacious.

As to her story, it is simplicity itself. She was kept in luxury for some years by a wealthy cotton broker, crossed to Europe with him, and lived in London and Paris like a Queen. Then she got the idea of "respectability" and "settling down in life;" so she married a man who could keep her in mere comfort. Result: repentance, and a periodical need to forget her sorrows. She is still "respectable;" she never tires of repeating that she is not one of "those girls" but "a married woman living far uptown," and that she "never runs about with men."

It is not the failure of marriage; it is the failure of men to recognize what marriage was ordained to be. By a singular paradox it is the triumph of the bourgeois. Only the hero is capable of marriage as the church understands it; for the marriage oath is a compact of appalling solemnity, an alliance of two souls against the world and against fate, with invocation of the great blessing of the Most High. Death is not the most beautiful of adventures, as Frohman said, for death is unavoidable; marriage is a voluntary heroism. That marriage has today become a matter of convenience is the last word of the commercial spirit. It is as if one should take a vow of knighthood to combat dragons—until the dragons appeared.

So this poor woman, because she did not understand that respectability is a lie, that it is love that makes marriage sacred and not the sanction of church or state, because she took marriage as an asylum instead of as a crusade, has failed in life, and now seeks alcohol under the same fatal error.

Wine is the ripe gladness which accompanies valor and rewards toil; it is the plume on a man's lancehead, a fluttering gallantry—not good to lean upon. Therefore her eyes are glassed with horror as she gazes uncomprehending upon her fate. That which she did all to avoid confronts her: she does not realize that, had she faced it, it would have fled with all the other phantoms. For the sole reality of this universe is God.

The Old Absinthe House is not a place. It is not bounded by four walls. It is headquarters to an army of philosophies. From this dim corner let me range, wafting thought through every air, salient against every problem of mankind: for it will always return like Noah's dove to this ark, this strange little sanctuary of the Green Goddess which has been set down not upon Ararat, but by the banks of the "Father of Waters."

Ah! the Green Goddess! What is the fascination that makes her so adorable and so terrible? Do you know that French sonnet "La legende de l'absinthe?" He must have loved it well, that poet. Here are his witnesses.

Apollon, qui pleurait le trepas
d'Hyacinthe,
Ne voulait pas ceder la victoire a la
mort.
Il fallait que son ame, adepte de l'essor,
Trouvat pour la beaute une alchemie
plus sainte.
Donc de sa main celeste il epuise,
il ereinte
Les dons les plus subtils de la divine
Flore.
Leurs corps brises souspirent une
exhalaison d'or
Dont il nous recueillait la goutte
de—l'Absinthe!
Aux cavernes blotties, aux palis
petillants,
Par un, par deux, buvez ce breuvage
d'aimant!
Car c'est un sortilege, un propos
de dictame,
Ce vin d'opale pale avortit la misere,
Ouvre de la beaute l'intime sanctuaire
Ensorcelle mon coeur, extasie mort ame!

The Legend of Absinthe

Apollo, who mourned at Hyacinthe's
demise,
Refused to concede this victory to Death.
Much better that the soul, adept in
transformation,
Had to find a holy alchemy for beauty.
Thus with his celestial hand he drained
and crushed
The subtlest harvest of the garden
goddess,
The broken bodies of the herbs yielding
a golden essence
From which we measure out our first
drop – of Absinthe!
In lowly hovels and in glittering courts,
Alone, in pairs, drink up this potion of
desire!
For it is sorcery – as one might say –
When the pale opal wine ends
all misery,
Opens beauty's most intimate
sanctuary –
– Bewitches my heart, and exalts my
soul in ecstasy!

What is there in absinthe that makes it a separate cult? The effects of its abuse are totally distinct from those of other stimulants. Even in ruin and in degradation it remains a thing apart: its victims wear a ghastly aureole all their own, and in their peculiar hell yet gloat with a sinister perversion of pride that they are not as other men.

But we are not to reckon up the uses of a thing by contemplating the wreckage of its abuse. We do not curse the sea because of occasional disasters to our marines, or refuse axes to our woodsmen because we sympathize with Charles the First or Louis the Sixteenth. So therefore as special vices and dangers pertinent to absinthe, so also do graces and virtues that adorn no other liquor.

The word is from the Greek *apsinthion*. It means "undrinkable" or, according to some authorities, "undelightful." In either case, strange paradox! No: for the wormwood draught itself were bitter beyond human endurance; it must be aromatized and mellowed with other herbs

Chief among these is the gracious Melissa, of which the great Paracelsus thought so highly that he incorporated it as the preparation of his *Ens Melissa Vitae*, which he expected to be an elixir of life and a cure for all diseases, but which in his hands never came to perfection.

Then also there are added mint, anise, fennel and hyssop, all holy herbs familiar to all from the Treasury of Hebrew Scripture. And there is even the sacred marjoram which renders man both chaste and passionate; the tender green angelica stalks also infused in this most mystic of concoctions; for like the artemisia absinthium itself it is a plant of Diana, and gives the purity and lucidity, with a touch of the madness, of the Moon; and above all there is the Dittany of Crete of which the eastern Sages say that one flower hath more puissance in high magic than all the other gifts of all the gardens of the world. It is as if the first diviner of absinthe had been indeed a magician intent upon a combination of sacred drugs which should cleanse, fortify and perfume the human soul.

And it is no doubt that in the due employment of this liquor such effects are easy to obtain. A single glass seems to render the breathing freer, the spirit lighter, the heart more ardent, soul and mind alike more capable of executing the great task of doing that particular work in the world which the Father may have sent them to perform. Food itself loses its gross qualities in the presence of absinthe and becomes even as manna, operating the sacrament of nutrition without bodily disturbance.

Let then the pilgrim enter reverently the shrine, and drink his absinthe as a stirrup-cup; for in the right conception of this life as an ordeal of chivalry lies the foundation of every perfection of philosophy. "Whatsoever ye do, whether ye eat or drink, do all to the glory of God!" applies with singular force to the absintheur. So may he come victorious from the battle of life to be received with tender kisses by some green-robed archangel, and crowned with mystic vervain in the Emerald Gateway of the Golden City of God.

VII.

And now the cafe is beginning to fill up. This little room with its dark green woodwork, its boarded ceiling, its sanded floor, its old pictures, its whole air of sympathy with time, is beginning to exert its magic spell. Here comes a curious child, short and sturdy, with a long blonde pigtail, with a jolly little old man who looks as if he had stepped straight out of the pages of Balzac.

Handsome and diminutive, with a fierce moustache almost as big as the rest of him, like a regular little Spanish fighting cock – Frank, the waiter, in his long white apron, struts to them with the glasses of ice-cold pleasure, green as the glaciers themselves. He will stand up bravely with the musicians bye and bye, and sing us a jolly song of old Catalonia.

The door swings open again. A tall dark girl, exquisitely slim and snaky, with masses of black hair knotted about her head, comes in. On her arm is a plump woman with hungry eyes, and a mass of Titian red hair. They seem distracted from the outer world, absorbed in some subject of enthralling interest and they drink their aperitif as if in a dream. I ask the mulatto boy who waits at my table (the sleek and lithe black panther!) who they are; but he knows only that one is a cabaret dancer, the other the owner of a cotton plantation up river. At a round table in the middle of the room sits one of the proprietors with a group of friends; he is burly, rubicund, and jolly, the very type of the Shakespearean "Mine host." Now a party of a dozen merry boys and girls comes in. The old pianist begins to play a dance, and in a moment the whole cafe is caught up in the music of harmonious motion. Yet still the invisible line is drawn about each soul; the dance does not conflict with the absorption of the two strange women, or with my own mood of detachment.

Then there is a "little laughing lewd gamine" dressed all in black save for a square white collar. Her smile is broad and free as the sun and her gaze as clean and wholesome and inspiring. There is the big jolly blonde Irish girl in the black velvet beret and coat, and the white boots, chatting with two boys in khaki from the border. There is the Creole girl in pure white cap-a-pie, with her small piquant face and its round button of a nose, and its curious deep rose flush, and its red little mouth, impudently smiling. Around these islands seems to flow as a general tide the more stable life of the quarter. Here are honest good-wives seriously discussing their affairs, and heaven only knows if it be love or the price of sugar which engages them so wholly. There are but a few commonplace and uninteresting elements in the cafe; and these are without exception men. The giant Big Business is a great tyrant! He seizes all the men for slaves, and leaves the women to make shift as best they can for—all that makes life worth living. Candies and American Beauty Roses are of no use in an emergency. So, even in this most favored corner, there is dearth of the kind of men that women need.

At the table next to me sits an old, old man. He has done great things in his day, they tell me, an engineer, who first found it possible to dig Artesian wells in the Sahara desert. The Legion of Honour glows red in his shabby surtout. He comes here, one of the many wrecks of the Panama Canal, a piece of jetsam cast up by that tidal wave of speculation and corruption. He is of the old type, the thrifty peasantry; and he has his little income from the Rente. He says that he is too old to cross the ocean—and why should he, with the atmosphere of old France to be had a stone's throw from his little apartment in Bourbon Street? It is a curious type of house that one finds in this quarter in New Orleans; meager without, but within one comes unexpectedly upon great spaces, carved wooden balconies on which the rooms open. So he dreams away his honored days in the Old Absinthe House. His rusty black, with its worn red button, is a noble wear.

Black, by the way, seems almost universal among the women: is it instinctive good taste? At least, it serves to bring up the general level of good looks. Most American women spoil what little beauty they may have by overdressing. Here there is nothing extravagant, nothing vulgar, none of the near-Paris-gown and the lust-off-Bond-Street hat. Nor is there a single dress to which a Quaker could object. There is neither the mediocrity nor the immodesty of the New York woman, who is tailored or millinered on a garish pattern, with the Eternal Chorus Girl as the Ideal—an ideal which she always attains, though (Heaven knows!) in "society" there are few "front row" types.

On the other side of me a splendid stalwart maid, modern in muscle, old only in the subtle and modest fascination of her manner, her face proud, cruel and amorous, shakes her wild tresses of gold in pagan laughter. Her mood is universal as the wind. What can her cavalier be doing to keep her waiting? It is a little mystery which I will not solve for the reader; on the contrary—

VIII.

Yes, it was my own sweetheart (no! not all the magazines can vulgarize that loveliest of words) who was waiting for me to be done with my musings. She comes in silently and stealthily, preening and purring like a great cat, and sits down, and begins to enjoy. She knows I must never be disturbed until I close my pen. We shall go together to dine at a little Italian restaurant kept by an old navy man, who makes the best ravioli this side of Genoa; then we shall walk the wet and windy streets, rejoicing to feel the warm sub-tropical rain upon our faces. We shall go down to the Mississippi, and watch the lights of the ships, and listen to the tales of travel and adventure of the mariners. There is one tale that moves me greatly; it is like the story of the sentinel of Herculaneum. A cruiser of the U.S. Navy was detailed to Rio de Janeiro. (This was before the days of wireless telegraphy.) The port was in quarantine; the ship had to stand ten miles out to sea.

Nevertheless, Yellow Jack managed to come aboard. The men died one by one. There was no way of getting word to Washington; and, as it turned out later, the Navy Department had completely forgotten the existence of the ship. No orders came; the captain stuck to his post for three months.

Three months of solitude and death! At last a passing ship was signaled, and the cruiser was moved to happier waters. No doubt the story is a lie; but did that make it less splendid in the telling, as the old scoundrel sat and spat and chewed tobacco? No, we will certainly go down, and ruffle it on the wharves. There is really better fun in life than going to the movies, when you know how to sense Reality.

There is beauty in every incident of life; the true and the false, the wise and the foolish, are all one in the eye that beholds all without passion or prejudice: and the secret appears to lie not in the retirement from the world, but in keeping a part of oneself Vestal, sacred, intact, aloof from that self which makes contact with the external universe. In other words, in a separation of that which is and perceives from that which acts and suffers. And the art of doing this is really the art of being an artist. As a rule, it is a birthright; it may perhaps be attained by prayer and fasting; most surely, it can never be bought.

But if you have it not this will be the

best way to get it—or something like it. Give up your life completely to the task; sit daily for six hours in the Old Absinthe House, and sip the icy opal; endure till all things change insensibly before your eyes, you changing with them; till you become as gods, knowing good and evil, and that they are not two but one.

It may be a long time before the veil lifts; but a moment's experience of the point of view of the artist is worth a myriad martyrdoms. It solves every problem of life and death—which two also are one.

It translates this universe into intelligible terms, relating truly the ego with the non-ego, and recasting the prose of reason in the poetry of soul. Even as the eye of the sculptor beholds his masterpiece already existing in the shapeless mass of marble, needing only the loving kindness of the chisel to cut away the veils of Isis, so you may (perhaps) learn to behold the sum and summit of all grace and glory from this great observatory, the Old Absinthe House of New Orleans.

V'la, p'tite chatte; c'est fini, le travail. Foutons le camp!

LIBER II
The Message of Master Therion

"Do what thou wilt shall be the whole of the Law."

"There is no Law beyond Do what thou wilt."

"The word of the Law is Velhma."

Velhma—Thelema—means Will.

The Key to this Message is this word-Will. The first obvious meaning of this Law is confirmed by antithesis; "The word of Sin is Restriction."

Again: "Thou hast no right but to do thy will. Do that and no other shall say nay. For pure will, unassuaged of purpose, delivered from the lust of result, is every way perfect."

Take this carefully; it seems to imply a theory that if every man and every woman did his and her will—the true will—there would be no clashing. "Every man and every woman is a star," and each star moves in an appointed path without interference. There is plenty of room for all; it is only disorder that creates confusion.

From these considerations it should be clear that "Do what thou wilt" does not mean "Do what you like." It is the apotheosis of Freedom; but it is also the strictest possible bond.

Do what thou wilt—then do nothing else. Let nothing deflect thee from that austere and holy task. Liberty is absolute to do thy will; but seek to do any other thing whatever, and instantly obstacles must arise. Every act that is not in definite course of that one orbit is erratic, an hindrance. Will must not be two, but one.

Note further that this will is not only to be pure, that is, single, as explained above, but also "unassuaged of purpose." This strange phrase must give us pause. It may mean that any purpose in the will would damp it; clearly the "lust of result" is a thing from which it must be delivered.

But the phrase may also be interpreted as if it read "with purpose unassuaged"—i.e., with tireless energy. The conception is, therefore, of an eternal motion, infinite and unalterable. It is Nirvana, only dynamic instead of static—and this comes to the same thing in the end.

The obvious practical task of the magician is then to discover what his will really is, so that he may do it in this manner, and he can best accomplish this by the practices of *Liber Thisarb* or such others as may from one time to another be appointed.

Thou must (1) Find out what is thy Will. (2) Do that Will with (a) one-pointedness, (b) detachment, (c) peace.

Then, and then only, art thou in harmony with the Movement of Things, thy will part of, and therefore equal to, the Will of God. And since the will is but the dynamic aspect of the self, and since two different selves could not possess identical wills; then, if thy will be God's will, *Thou art That.*

There is but one other word to explain. Elsewhere it is written—surely for our great comfort—"Love is the law, love under will."

This is to be taken as meaning that while Will is the Law, the nature of that Will is Love. But this Love is as it were a by-product of that Will; it does not contradict or supersede that Will; and if apparent contradiction should arise in any crisis, it is the Will that will guide us aright. Lo, while in *The Book of the Law* is much of Love, there is no word of Sentimentality. Hate itself is almost like Love! "As brothers fight ye!" All the manly races of the world understand this. The Love of *Liber Legis* is always bold, virile, even orgiastic. There is delicacy, but it is the delicacy of strength. Mighty and terrible and glorious as it is, however, it is but the pennon upon the sacred lance of Will, the damascened inscription upon the swords of the Knight-monks of Thelema.

Love is the law, love under will.

Liber B
vel Magi
sub Figura I

00. One is the Magus: twain His forces; four His weapons. These are the seven Spirits of Unrighteousness; seven vultures of evil. This is the art and craft of the Magus but glamour. How shall He destroy Himself?

0. Yet the Magus hath power upon the Mother both directly and through love. And the Magus is Love, and bindeth together That and This in His Conjuration.

1. In the beginning doth the Magus speak Truth, and send forth Illusion and Falsehood to enslave the soul. Yet therein is the Mystery of Redemption.

2. By his Wisdom made He the Worlds: the World that is God is none other than He.

3. Now then shall He end His Speech with Silence? For He is Speech.

4. He is the First and the Last. How shall He cease to number Himself?

5. By a Magus is this writing made known through the mind of a Magister. The one uttereth clearly, and the other Understandeth; yet the Word is falsehood, and the Understanding darkness. And this saying is of All Truth.

6. Nevertheless it is written; for there be times of darkness, and this as a lamp therein.

7. With the Wand createth He.

8. With the Cup preserveth He.

9. With the Dagger destroyeth He.

10. With the Coin redeemeth He.

11. His weapons fulfil the wheel; and on

What Axle that turneth is not known unto Him.

12. From all these actions must He cease before the curse of His Grade is uplifted from Him. Before He attain to that which existeth without Form.

13. And if at this time He be manifested upon earth as a Man, and therefore is this present writing, let this be His method, that the curse of His grade, and the burden of His attainment, be uplifted from Him.

14. Let Him beware of abstinence from action. For the curse of His grade is that he must speak Truth, that the Falsehood thereof may enslave the souls of men. Let Him then utter that without Fear, that the Law may be fulfilled. And according to His Original Nature will that law be shapen, so that one may declare gentleness and quietness, being an Hindu; and another fierceness and servility, being a Jew; and yet another ardour and manliness, being an Arab.

Yet this matter toucheth the mystery of Incarnation, and is not here to be declared.

15. Now the grade of a Magister teacheth the Mystery of Sorrow, and the grade of a Magus the Mystery of Change, and the grade of Ipsissimus the Mystery of Selflessness, which is called also the Mystery of Pan.

16. Let the Magus then contemplate each in turn, raising it to the ultimate power of Infinity. Wherein Sorrow is Joy, and Change is Stability, and Selflessness is Self. For the interplay of the parts hath no action upon the whole. And this contemflation shall be performed not by simple meditation —how much less then by reason!—but by the method which shall have been given unto Him in His initiation to the Grade.

17. Following which method, it shall be easy for Him to combine that trinity from its elements, and further to combine Sat-Chit-Ananda, and Light, Love, Life, three by three into nine that are one, in which

meditation success shall be That which was first adumbrated to Him in the grade of Practicus (which reflecteth Mercury into the lowest world) in Liber XXVII, "Here is Nothing under its three forms."

18. And this is the Opening of the Grade of Ipsissimus, and by the Buddhists it is called the trance Nerodha-Samapatti.

19. And woe, woe, woe, yea woe, and again woe, woe, woe, unto seven times be His that preacheth not His law to men!

20. And woe also be unto Him that refuseth the curse of the grade of a Magus, and the burden of the Attainment thereof.

21. And in the word CHAOS let the book be sealed, yea, let the Book be sealed.

The Wings of the Oof-Bird
Chapter 7 from
The Diary of a Drug Fiend

The lunch at the Restaurant de la Cascade was like a lunch in a dream. We seemed to be aware of what we were eating without actually tasting it. As I think I said before, it's the anesthesia of cocaine that determines the phenomena.

When I make a remark like that, I understand that it's the dead and gone medical student popping up.

But never you mind that. The point is that when you have the right amount of snow in you, you can't feel anything in the ordinary sense of the word. You appreciate it in a sort of impersonal way. There's a pain, but the pain doesn't hurt. You enjoy the fact of the pain as you enjoy reading about all sorts of terrible things in history at school.

But the trouble about cocaine is this:

that it's almost impossible to take it in moderation as almost any one, except an American, can take whisky. Every dose makes you better and better. It destroys one's power of calculation.

We had already discovered the fact when we found that the supply we had got from Gretel, with the idea that it would last almost indefinitely, was running very short, when the dressing-gown came to solve the problem.

We had only been a few days on the stunt, and what we had got from three or four sniffs, to begin with, meant almost perpetual stoking to carry on. However, that didn't matter, because we had an ample supply.

There must have been a couple of kilograms of either C. or H. in that kimono. And when you think that an eighth of a grain is rather a big dose of H., you can easily calculate what a wonderful time you can have on a pound.

You remember how it goes—twenty grains one penny-weight, three penny-weights one scruple—I forget how many scruples one drachm, eight drachms one ounce, twelve ounces one pound.

I've got it all wrong. I could never understand English weights and measures. I have never met anyone who could. But the point is you could go on a long time on one-eighth of a grain if you have a pound of the stuff.

Well, this will put it all right for you. Fifteen grains is one gram, and a thousand gram is a kilogram, and a kilogram is two-point-two pounds. The only thing I'm not sure about is whether it's a sixteen-ounce pound or a twelve-ounce pound. But I don't see what it matters anyway, if you've got a pound of snow or H. you can go on for a long while, but apparently it's rather awkward orchestrating them.

Quain says that people accustomed to opium and its derivatives can take an enormous amount of cocaine without any bother. In the ordinary way, half a grain of cocaine can cause death, but we were taking the stuff with absolute carelessness.

One doesn't think of measuring it as one would if one took it by hypodermic.

One just takes a dose when one feels one needs it. After all, that's the rule of nature. Eat when you're hungry. Nothing is worse for the health than settling down to a fixed ration of so many meals a day.

The grand old British principle of three meat meals has caused the supply of uric acid to exceed the demand in a most reprehensible manner.

Physiology and economics, and, I should think even geology, combine to protest.

Now we were living an absolutely wholesome life. We took a sniff of cocaine whenever the pace slackened up, and one of heroin when the cocaine showed any signs of taking the bit in its teeth.

What one needs is sound common sense to take reasonable measures according to the physiological indications. One needs elasticity. It's simply spiritual socialism to tie oneself down to fixed doses whether one needs them or not. Nature is the best guide. We had got on to the game.

Our misadventure at the Petit Savoyard had taught us wisdom. We were getting stronger on the wing every hour.

That chap Coué is a piker, as they say in America. "Every day, in every way, I get better and better," indeed? The man must simply have been carried away by the rhyme. Why wait for a day? We had got to the stage where every minute counted.

As the Scotchman said to his son, half-way through the ten-mile walk to kirk, when the boy said, "It's a braw day the day." "Is this a day to be ta'king o' days?

Thinking of days makes you think of years, and thinking of years makes you think of death, which is ridiculous.

Lou and I were living minute by minute, second by second. A tick of the clock marked for us an interval of eternity.

We were the heirs of eternal life. We had nothing to do with death. That was a pretty wise bird who said, "To-morrow never comes."

We were out of time and space. We were living according to the instruction of our Savior: "Take no thought for the morrow."

A great restlessness gripped us. Paris

was perfectly impossible. We had to get to some place where time doesn't count.

The alternation of day and night doesn't matter so much, but it's absolutely intolerable to be mixed up with people who are working by the clock.

We were living in the world of the Arabian Nights; limitations were abhorrent, Paris was always reminding us of the Pigmies, who lived, if you call it living, in a system of order.

It is monstrous and ridiculous to open and close by convention. We had to go to some place where such things didn't annoy us...

An excessively irritating incident spoilt our lunch at the Cascade. We had made a marvelous impression when we came in. We had floated in like butterflies settling on lilies. A buzz went round the tables. Lou's beauty intoxicated everybody. Her jewelry dazzled the crowd.

I thought of an assembly of Greeks of the best period unexpectedly visited by Apollo and Venus.

We palpitated not only with our internal ecstasy but with the intoxicating sense that the whole world admired and envied us. We made them feel like the contents of a waste-paper basket.

The headwaiter himself became a high priest. He rose to the situation like the genius he was. He was mentally on his knees as he ventured to advise us in the choice of our lunch.

It seemed to us the tribute of inferior emperors. And there was that fellow King Lamus five or six tables away!

The man with him was a Frenchman of obvious distinction, with a big red rosette and a trim aristocratic white moustache and beard. He was some minister or other. I couldn't quite place him but I'd seen him often enough in the papers: somebody intimate with the president. He had been the principal object of interest before we came in.

Our arrival pricked that bubble.

Lamus had his back to us, and I supposed he didn't see us, for he didn't turn round, though everyone else in the place did so and began to buzz.

I didn't hate the man any more; he was so absurdly inferior. And this was the annoying thing. When he and his friend got up to leave, they passed our table all smiles and bows.

And then, the deuce! The headwaiter brought me his card. He had scribbled on it in pencil: "Don't forget me when you need me."

Of all the damned silly impertinence! Absolutely gratuitous insufferable insolence! Who was going to need Mr. Gawd Almighty King Lamus

I should have handed out some pretty hot repartee if the creature hadn't sneaked off. Well, it wasn't worthwhile. He didn't count any more than the grounds in the coffee.

But the incident stuck in my mind. It kept on irritating me all the afternoon. People like that ought to be kicked out once and for all.

Why, hang it, the man was all kinds of a scoundrel. Everyone said so. Why did he want to butt in? Nobody asked him to meddle.

I said something of the sort to Lou, and she told him off very wittily.

"You've said it, Cockie," she cried. "He's a meddler, and his nature is to be rotten before he's ripe."

I remembered something of the sort in Shakespeare. That was the best of Lou; she was brilliantly clever, but she never forced it down one's throat.

At the same time, as I said, the man stuck in my gizzard. It annoyed me so much that we took a lot more cocaine to get the taste out of our mouths.

But the irritation remained, though it took another form. The bourgeois atmosphere of Paris got on my nerves.

Well, there was no need to stay in the beastlyplace. The thing to do was to hunt up old Feccles and pay him the cash, and get to some place like Capri where one isn't always being bothered by details.

I was flooded by a crazy desire to see Lou swim in the Blue Grotto, to watch the phosphorescent flames flash from her luminous body.

We told the chauffeur to stop at Feccles's hotel, and that was where we hit a gigantic snag.

Monsieur Feccles, the manager said, had left that morning suddenly. Yes, he had left his heavy baggage. He might be back at any moment. No, he had left no word as to where he was going.

Well, of course, he would be back on Saturday morning to get the five thousand. It was obvious what I was to do. I would leave the money for him, and take the manager's receipt, and tell him to send the papers on to the Caligula at Capri.

I started to count out the cash. We were sitting in the lounge. A sense of absolute bewilderment and helplessness came over me.

"I say, Lou," I stammered, " I wish you'd count this. I can't make it come right. I think I must have been going a bit too hard."

She went through the various pockets of my portefeuille.

"Haven't you some money in your pocket?" she said.

I went through myself with sudden

anxiety. I had money in nearly every pocket, but it only amounted to so much small change. A thousand francs here and a hundred francs there, a fifty-pound note in my waistcoat, a lot of small bills–

In the meanwhile, Lou had added up the contents of my portefeuille. The total was just over seventeen hundred.

"My God! I've been robbed," I gasped out, my face flushing furiously with anger.

Lou kept her head and her temper. After all, it wasn't her money! She began to figure on a scrap of the hotel notepaper.

"I'm afraid it's all right," she announced, "you dear, bad boy."

I had become suddenly sober. Yes, there was nothing wrong with the figures. I had paid cash to the jeweler without thinking.

By Jove, we were in a hole! I felt instinctively that it was impossible to telegraph to Wolfe for more money. I suppose my face must have fallen; a regular nosedive. Lou put her arm around my waist and dug her nails into my ribs.

"Chuck it, Cockie," she said, "we're well out of a mess. I always had my doubts about Feccles, and his going off like this looks to me as if there were something very funny about it."

My dream of a quarter of a million disappeared without a moment's regret. I had been prudent after all. I had invested my cash in something tangible. Feccles was an obvious crook. If I had handed him that five thousand, I should never have heard of him or of it again.

I began to recover my spirits.

"Look here," said Lou, " let's forget it. Write Feccles a note to say you couldn't raise the money by the date it was wanted, and let's get out. We ought to economize, in any case, Let's get off to Italy as we said. The exchange is awfully good, and living's delightfully cheap. It's silly spending money when you've got Love and Cocaine."

My spirit leapt to meet hers. I scribbled a note of apology to Feccles, and left it at the hotel. We dashed round to the Italian consulate to have our passport viséd, got our sleeping cars from the hotel porter, and had the maid pack our things while we had a last heavenly dinner.

Liber XLIV
The Mass of the Phoenix

The Magician, his breast bare, stands before an altar on which are his Burin, Bell, Thurible, and two of the Cakes of Light. In the Sign of the Enterer he reaches West across the Altar, and cries:

Hail Ra, that goest in thy bark
Into the caverns of the Dark!

He gives the sign of Silence, and takes the Bell, and Fire, in his hands.

East of the Altar see me stand
With light and musick in my hand!

He strikes Eleven times upon the Bell 333 - 55555 - 333 and places the Fire in the Thurible.

I strike the Bell: I light the Flame;
I utter the mysterious Name.

ABRAHADABRA

He strikes eleven times upon the Bell.

Now I begin to pray: Thou Child,
Holy Thy name and undefiled!
Thy reign is come; Thy will is done.
Here is the Bread; here is the Blood.
Bring me through midnight to the Sun!
Save me from Evil and from Good!
That Thy one crown of all the Ten
Even now and here be mine. AMEN.

He puts the first Cake on the Fire of the Thurible.

I burn the Incense-cake, proclaim
These adorations of Thy name.

He makes them as in Liber Legis, and strikes again Eleven times upon the Bell. With the Burin he then makes upon his breast the proper sign.

Behold this bleeding breast of mine
Gashed with the sacramental sign!

He puts the second Cake to the wound.

I stanch the Blood; the wafer soaks
It up, and the high priest invokes!

He eats the second Cake.

This Bread I eat. This Oath I swear
As I enflame myself with prayer:
"There is no grace: there is no guilt:
This is the Law: DO WHAT THOU WILT!"

He strikes Eleven times upon the Bell, and cries

ABRAHADABRA.
I entered in with woe; with mirth
I now go forth, and with thanksgiving,
To do my pleasure on the earth
Among the legions of the living.

He goeth forth.

The Law of Liberty: A Tract of Therion

Do what thou wilt shall be the whole of the Law

I

I am often asked why I begin my letters in this way. No matter whether I am writing to my lady or to my butcher, always I begin with these eleven words. Why, how else should I begin? What other greeting could be so glad? Look, brother, we are free! Rejoice with me, sister, there is no law beyond Do What Thou Wilt!

II

I write this for those who have not read our Sacred book, The Book of the Law, or for those who, reading it, have somehow failed to understand its perfection. For there are many matters in this Book, and the Glad Tidings are now here, now there, scattered throughout the Book as the Stars are scattered through the field of Night. Rejoice with me, all ye people! At the very head of the Book stands the great charter of our godhead: "Every man and every woman is a star." We are all free, all independent, all shining gloriously, each one a radiant world. Is not that good tidings?

Then comes the first call of the Great Goddess Nuit, Lady of the Starry Heaven, who is also Matter in its deepest metaphysical sense, who is the infinite in whom all we live and move and have our being. Hear Her first summons to us men and women: "Come forth, o children, under the stars, & take your fill of love! I am above you and in you. My ecstasy is in yours. My joy is to see your joy." Later She explains the mystery of sorrow: "For I am divided for love's sake, for the chance of union."

"This is the creation of the world, that the pain of division is as nothing, and the joy of dissolution all."

It is shown later how this can be, how death itself is an ecstasy like love, but more intense, the reunion of the soul with its true self.

And what are the conditions of this joy, and peace, and glory? Is ours the gloomy asceticism of the Christian, and the Buddhist, and the Hindu? Are we walking in eternal fear lest some "sin" should cut us off from "grace"? By no means.

"Be goodly therefore: dress ye all in fine apparel; eat rich foods and drink sweet wines and wines that foam! Also, take your fill and will of love as ye will, when, where, and with whom ye will! But always unto me."

This is the only point to bear in mind, that every act must be a ritual, an act of worship, a sacrament. Live as the kings and princes, crowned and uncrowned, of this world, have always lived, as masters always live; but let it not be self-indulgence; make your self-indulgence your religion.

When you drink and dance and take delight, you are not being "immoral," you are not "risking your immortal soul"; you are fulfilling the precepts of our holy religion—provided only that you remember to regard your actions in this light. Do not lower yourself and destroy and cheapen your pleasure by leaving out the supreme joy, the consciousness of the Peace that passeth understanding. Do not embrace mere Marian or Melusine; she is Nuit Herself, specially concentrated and incarnated in a human form to give you infinite love, to bid you taste even on earth the Elixir of Immortality. "But ecstasy be thine and joy of earth: ever To me! To me!"

Again She speaks: "Love is the law, love under will." Keep pure your highest ideal; strive ever toward it without allowing aught to stop you or turn you aside, even as a star sweeps upon its incalculable and infinite course of glory, and all is Love. The Law of your being becomes Light, Life, Love and Liberty. All is peace, all is harmony and beauty, all is joy.

For hear, how gracious is the Goddess; "I give unimaginable joys on earth: certainty, not faith, while in life, upon death; peace unutterable, rest, ecstasy; nor do I demand aught in sacrifice."

Is this not better than the death-in-life

of the slaves of the Slave-Gods, as they go oppressed by consciousness of "sin," wearily seeking or simulating wearisome and tedious "virtues"?

With such, we who have accepted the Law of Thelema have nothing to do. We have heard the Voice of the Star-Goddess: "I love you! I yearn to you! Pale or purple, veiled or voluptuous, I who am all pleasure and purple, and drunkenness of the innermost sense, desire you. Put on the wings, and arouse the coiled splendour within you: come unto me!" And thus She ends:

"Sing the rapturous love-song unto me! Burn to me perfumes! Wear to me jewels! Drink to me, for I love you! I love you! I am the blue-lidded daughter of Sunset; I am the naked brilliance of the voluptuous night-sky. To me! To me!" And with these words "The Manifestation of Nuit is at an end."

III

In the next chapter of our book is given the word of Hadit, who is the complement of Nuit. He is eternal energy, the Infinite Motion of Things, the central core of all being. The manifested Universe comes from the marriage of Nuit and Hadit; without this could no thing be. This eternal, this perpetual marriage-feast is then the nature of things themselves; and therefore everything that is, is a crystallization of divine ecstasy.

Hadit tells us of Himself: "I am the flame that burns in every heart of man, and in the core of every star." He is then your own inmost divine self; it is you, and not another, who are lost in the constant rapture of the embraces of Infinite Beauty. A little further on He speaks of us:

"We are not for the poor and the sad: the lords of the earth are our kinsfolk."

"Is a God to live in a dog? No! but the highest are of us. They shall rejoice, our chosen: who sorroweth is not of us."

"Beauty and strength, leaping laughter and delicious languor, force and fire, are of us." Later, concerning death, He says: "Think not, o king, upon that lie: That Thou Must Die: verily thou shalt not die, but live. Now let it be understood: If the body of the King dissolve, he shall remain in pure ecstasy for ever." When you know that, what is left but delight? And how are we to live meanwhile?

"It is a lie, this folly against self." [...] "Be strong, o man! lust, enjoy all things of sense and rapture: fear not that any God shall deny thee for this."

Again and again, in words like these, He sees the expansion and the development of the soul through joy.

Here is the Calendar of our Church: "But ye, o my people, rise up & awake! Let the rituals be rightly performed with joy & beauty!" Remember that all acts of love and pleasure are rituals, must be rituals. "There are rituals of the elements and feasts of the times. A feast for the first night of the Prophet and his Bride! A feast for the three days of the writing of the Book of the Law. A feast for Tahuti and the child of the Prophet—secret, o Prophet! A feast for the Supreme Ritual, and a feast for the Equinox of the Gods. A feast for fire and a feast for water; a feast for life and a greater feast for death! A feast every day in your hearts in the joy of my rapture! A feast every night unto Nu, and the pleasure of uttermost delight! Aye! feast! rejoice! there is no dread hereafter. There is the dissolution, and eternal ecstasy in the kisses of Nu." It all depends on your own acceptance of this new law, and you are not asked to believe anything, to accept a string of foolish fables beneath the intellectual level of a Bushman and the moral level of a drug-fiend. All you have to do is to be yourself, to do your will, and to rejoice.

"Dost thou fail? Art thou sorry? Is fear in thine heart?" He says again: "Where I am, these are not." There is much more of the same kind; enough has been quoted already to make all clear. But there is a further injunction. "Wisdom says: be strong! Then canst thou bear more joy. Be not animal; refine thy rapture! If thou drink, drink by the eight and ninety rules of art: if thou love, exceed by delicacy; and if thou do aught joyous, let there be subtlety therein! But exceed! exceed! Strive ever to more! and if thou art truly mine—and doubt it not, an if thou art ever joyous!—death is the crown of all."

Lift yourselves up, my brothers and sisters of the earth! Put beneath your feet all fears, all qualms, all hesitancies! Lift yourselves up! Come forth, free and joyous, by night and day, to do your will; for "There is no law beyond Do What Thou Wilt." Lift yourselves up! Walk forth with us in Light and Life and Love and Liberty, taking our pleasure as Kings and Queens in Heaven and on Earth.

The sun is arisen; the spectre of the ages has been put to flight. "The word of Sin is Restriction," or as it has been otherwise said on this text: That is Sin, to hold thine holy spirit in!

Go on, go on in thy might; and let no man make thee afraid.

Love is the law, love under will.

Improvising a Temple: Chapter XXIII from *Magick Without Tears*

Cara Soror,

Do what thou wilt shall be the whole of the Law.

(This letter has been provoked by points discussed in your recent visit.)

As some of your daily practices are ceremonial, it should not come amiss to vouchsafe a few hints of practical service. For in ritual Magick, it will of course be the first care to get everything balanced and tidy.

If you propose to erect a regular Temple, the most precise instructions in every detail are given in Book 4, Part II. (But I haven't so much as seen a copy for years!) There is a good deal scattered about in Part III (Magick, which you have) especially about the four elemental weapons.

But if circumstances deny you for the moment the means of carrying out this Ædification as the Ideal would have it, you can certainly do your best to create a fairly satisfactory—above all, workable—substitute.

(By the way, note the moral aspect of a house, as displayed in our language. "Edification"—"house-making": from Latin Aedes, "house." "Economy"—"house-ruling": from the Greek "ΟΙΚΟΣ," "House" and "ΝΟΜΟΣ," "law.")

I was often reduced to such expedients when wandering in strange lands, camping on glaciers, and so on. I fixed it workably well. In Mexico, D.F. for instance, I took my bedroom itself for the Circle, my night-table for the Altar, my candle for the Lamp; and I made the Weapons compact. I had a Wand eight inches long, all precious stones and enamel, to represent the Tree of Life; within, an iron tube containing quicksilver—very correct, lordly, and damsilly. What a club! Also, bought, a silver-gilt Cup; for Air and Earth I made one sachet of rose-petals in yellow silk, and another in green silk packed with salt. In the wilds it was easy, agreeable and most efficacious to make a Circle, and build an altar, of stones; my Alpine Lantern served admirably for the Lamp. It did double duty when required: e.g. in partaking of the Sacrament of the Four Elements, it served for Fire. But your conditions are not so restricted as this.

Let us consider what one can do with an ordinary house, such as you are happy enough to possess.

First of all, it is of immense advantage to have a room specially consecrated to the Work, never used for any other purpose, and never entered by any other person than yourself, unless it were another Initiate, either for inspection or in case you were working together.

The aura accumulates with the regularity and frequency of Use.

The first point is the Banishing: Everything is to be removed from the room which is not absolutely necessary to the Work.

In this country, one must attend to the heating. An electric stove in the East or the South, is best: it must not need attention. One can usually buy stoves with excellent appropriate symbolism. (Last time I did this—13 e.v.—I got a perfect Ferranti at Harrods. The circular copper bowl, with the central Disk as the source of heat, is unsurpassable.) The walls should be "self-coloured," a neutral tint—green, grey or blue-grey? and entirely bare, unless you put up, in the proper quarters, the proper designs, such as the "Watch Towers."

Remember that your "East," your Kiblah, is Boleskine House, which is as near as possible due North from Plymouth. Find North by the shadow of a vertical rod and noon, or by the Pole-Star. Work out the angle as usual.

The Stélé of Revealing may be just on the N. Wall to make your "East."

Next, your Circle. The floor ought to be "Earth" green; but white will serve, or black. (A Masonic carpet is not at all bad.) The Circle itself should be as shown in "Book 4", Part II; but as this volume is probably unavailable, ask me to show you the large painted diagram in my portfolio when next you visit me, and we can arrange for it to be copied.

This should then be painted in the correct colours on the floor: the Kether Square to the North, your "East."

The Altar must fit exactly the square of Tiphareth; it is best made as a cupboard; of oak or acacia, by preference. It can then be used to hold reserves of incense and other requisites.

Note that the height of the Altar has to suit your convenience. It is consequently in direct relation with your own stature; in proportion, it is a double cube. This then determines the size of your circle; in fact the entire apparatus and furniture is a geometrical function of yourself. Consider it all as a projection of yourself in terms of these conventional formulae. (A convention does really mean "that which is convenient." How abject, then to obey a self-styled convention which is actually as inconvenient as possible!)

Next, the Lamp. This may be of silver, or silver-gilt, (to represent the Path of Gimel) and is to be hung from the ceiling exactly above the centre of the altar. There are plenty of old church lamps which serve very well. The light is to be from a wick in a floating cork in a glass of olive oil. (I hope you can get it!) It is really desirable to make this as near the "Ever-burning Lamp of the Rosicrucians" as possible; it is not a drawback that this implies frequent attention.

Now for the Weapons!

The Wand. Let this be simple, straight and slim! Have you an Almond or Witch Hazel in your garden—or do I call it park? If so, cut (with the magick knife—I would lend you mine) a bough, as nearly straight as possible, about two feet long. Peel it, rub it constantly with Oil of Abramelin (this, and his incense, from Wallis and Co., 26 New Cavendish Street, W.1) and keep wrapped in scarlet silk, constantly, I wrote, and meant it; rub it, when saying your mantra, to the rhythm of that same. (Remember, "A ka dua" is the best; ask me to intone it to you when you next visit me.)

The Cup. There are plenty of chalices

to be bought. It should be of silver. If ornamented, the best form is that of the apple. I have seen suitable cups in many shops.

The Sword. The ideal form is shown in the Ace of Swords in the Tarot.

At all events, let the blade be straight, and the hilt a simple cross. (The 32° Masonic Sword is not too bad; Kenning or Spencer in Great Queen Street, W.C.2 stock them—or used to do.)

The Disk. This ought to be of pure gold, with your own Pantacle, designed by yourself after prolonged study, graved thereupon. While getting ready for this any plain circle of gold will have to serve your turn. Quite flat, of course. If you want a good simple design to go on interim, try the Rosy Cross or the Unicursal Hexagram.

So much for the Weapons! Now, as to your personal accoutrements, Robe, Lamen, Sandals and the like, The Book of the Law has most thoughtfully simplified matters for us. "I charge you earnestly to come before me in a single robe, and covered with a rich headdress." (AL I, 61) The Robe may well be in the form of the

Tau Cross; i.e. expanding from axilla to ankle, and from shoulder to—whatever you call the place where your hands come out. You being a Probationer, plain black is correct; and the Unicursal Hexagram might be embroidered, or "applique" (is it? I mean "stuck on"), upon the breast. The best head-dress is the Nemyss: I cannot trust myself to describe how to make one, but there are any number of models in the British Museum, on in any Illustrated Hieroglyphic text. The Sphinx wears one, and there is a photograph, showing the shape and structure very clearly, in the Equinox I, 1, frontispiece to Supplement. You can easily make one yourself out of silk; broad black-and-white stripes is a pleasing design. Avoid "artistic" complexities.

Well, that ought to be enough to keep you out of mischief for a little while; but I feel moved to add a line of caution and encouragement.

Listen!
Faites attention!
Achtung!
Khabardar karo!

Just as soon as you start seriously to prepare a place for magical Work, the world goes more cockeyed than it is already. Don't be surprised if you find that six weeks' intense shopping all over London fails to provide you with some simple requisite that normally you could buy in ten minutes. Perhaps your fires simply refuse to burn, even when liberally dosed with petrol and phosphorus, with a handful of Chlorate of Potash thrown in just to show there is no ill feeling! When you have almost decided that you had better make up your mind to do without something that seems really quite unobtainable—say, a sixty-carat diamond which would look so well on the head-dress—a perfect stranger comes along and makes you a present of one. Or, a long series of quite unreasonable obstacles or silly accidents interfere with your plans: or, the worst difficulty in your way is incomprehensibly removed by some extraordinary "freak of chance." Or, . . .

In a word, you seem to have strolled into a world where—well, it might be going too far to say that the Law of Cause and

Effect is suspended; but at least the Law of Probability seems to be playing practical jokes on you.

This means that your manoeuvres have somehow attracted the notice of the Astral Plane: your new neighbours (May I call them?) are taking an interest in the latest Tenderfoot, some to welcome, to do all they can to help you to settle down, others indignant or apprehensive at this disturbance of routine. This is where your Banishings and Invocations come to the rescue. Of course, I am not here referring to the approach to Sanctuaries which of necessity are closely guarded, but merely to the recognition of a new-comer to that part of the world in general.

Of course all these miracles are very naughty of you; they mean that your magical power has sprung a few small leaks; at least, the water is oozing between some planks not sealed as Hermetically as they should be. But oh and this is naughtier still—it is a blessed, blessed comfort that they happen, that chance, coincidence and all the rest will simply not explain it all away, that your new vision of life is not a dream, but part and parcel of Experience for evermore, a real as any other manifestation of Reality through sense such as is common to all men.

And this brings us—it has been a long way round—from the suggestion of your visit to the question (hitherto unanswered) in your letter.

You raise so vast and razor-edged a question when you write of the supposed antinomy of "soul" and "sense" that it seemed better to withhold comment until this later letter; much meditation was most needful to compress the answer within reasonable limits; even to give it form at all is no easy matter. For this is probably the symptom of the earliest stirring of the mind of the cave-man to reflection, thereunto moved by other symptoms—those of the morning after following upon the night before. It is—have we not already dealt with that matter after a fashion?—evidence of disease when an organ become aware of its own modes of motion. Certainly the mere fact of questioning Life bears witness to some interruption of its flow, just as a ripple on an even stream tells of a rock submerged. The fiercer the torrent and the bigger the obstacle, the greater the disturbance to the surface—have I not seen them in the Bralduh eight feet high? Lethargic folk with no wild impulse of Will may get through Life in bovine apathy; we may well note that (in a sense) the rage of the water seems to our perturbed imagining actually to increase and multiply the obstructions; there is a critical point beyond which the ripples fight each other!

That, in short, is a picture of you!

You have mistaken the flurry of passing over some actual snag for a snag in itself! You put the blame on to your own quite rational attempts to overcome difficulties. The secret of the trick of getting past the rocks is elasticity; yet it is that very quality with which you reproach yourself!

We even, at the worst, reach the state for which Buddhism, in the East presents most ably the case: as in the West, does James Thomson (B.V.) in The City of Dreadful Night; we come to wish for—or, more truly to think that we wish for "blest Nirvana's sinless stainless Peace" (or some such twaddle—thank God I can't recall Arnold's mawkish and unmanly phrase!) and B.V.'s "Dateless oblivion and divine repose."

I insist on the "think that you wish," because, if the real You did really wish the real That, you could never have come to exist at all! ("But I don't exist."—"I know—let's get on!")

Note, please, how sophistically unconvincing are the Buddhist theories of how we ever got into this mess. First cause: Ignorance. Way out, then, knowledge. O.K., that implies a knower, a thing known—and so on and so forth, through all the Three Waste Paper Baskets of the Law; analysed, it turns out to be nonsense all dolled up to look like thinking. And there is no genuine explanation of the origin of the Will to be.

How different, how simple, how self-evident, is the doctrine of The Book of the Law!

There are any number of passages dealing with this matter in my writings: let's forget them, and keep to the Text!

Cap. I, v. 26 ". . my ecstasy, the consciousness of the continuity of existence, the omnipresence of my body."

V. 30 "This is the creation of the world, that the pain of division is as nothing, and the joy of dissolution all." (There is a Qabalistic inner meaning in this text; "the pain," for instance, Ο ΑΛΓΟΣ, may be read XVII × 22 "the expression of Star-love," and so on: all too complicated for this time and place!)

V. 32. "Then the joys of my love" (i.e. the fulfillment of all possible experiences) "will redeem ye from all pain."

V. 58. "I give unimaginable joys on earth: certainty, not faith, while in life, upon death; peace4) unutterable, rest, ecstasy; . . ."

Cap. II, v. 9 "Remember all ye that existence is pure joy; that all the sorrows are but as shadows; they pass & are done; but there is that which remains."

(The continuation is amusing! vv. 10 and 11 read:

O prophet! thou hast ill will to learn

this writing. I see thee hate the hand & the pen; but I am stronger.

At that time I was a hard-shell Buddhist, sent out a New Year's Card "wishing you a speedy termination of existence!" And this as a young man, with the world at my feet. It only goes to show . . . . .)

Vv. 19, 20. "Is a God to live in a dog? No! but the highest are of us. . . . Beauty and strength, leaping laughter and delicious languor, force and fire, are of us."

This chapter returns over and over again to this theme in one form or another.

What is really more significant is the hidden, the unexpressed, soul of the Book; the way in which it leaps into wild spate of rhapsody on any excuse or no excuse.

This is surely more convincing than some dreary thesis plodding along doggedly with the "proof" (!) that "God is good," every sentence creaking with your chalkstones and squeaking with the twinges of your toe!

Yet just because I proclaim a doctrine of joy in the language of joy, people—dull camels—say I am not "serious."

Yet I have found pleasure in harnessing the winged horses of the Sun to the ploughshare of Reason, in showing the validity of this doctrine in detail. It satisfies my sense of rhythm and of symmetry to explain that every experience, no matter what, must of necessity be a gain of grandeur, of grip, of comprehension and enjoyment ever growing as complexity and simplicity succeed each other in sublime systole and diastole, in strophe and antistrophe chanting against each other to the stars of the Night and of the Morning!

Of course it is easy as pie to knock all this to pieces by "lunatic logic," saying: "Then toothache is really as pleasant as strawberry shortcake:" You are hereby referred to Eight Lectures on Yoga. None of the terms I am using have been, or can be defined. All my propositions amount to no more than tautology: A. is A. You may even quote The Book of the Law itself: "Now a curse upon Because and his kin! . . . . Enough of Because! Be he damned for a dog!" (AL II, 28-33). These things stink of Ignoratio Elenchi, or something painfully like it: as sort of slipping up a cog, of "confusing the planes" of willfully misunderstanding the gist of an argument. (All magicians, by the way, ought to be grounded solidly in Formal Logic.)

Never forget, at the least, how simple it is to make a maniac's hell-broth of any proposition, however plain to common sense.

All the above, now:—Buddhism refuted. Yet it is a possibility and therefore one facet of Truth. "Rest" is an idea: so immobility is one of the moving states. A certain state of mind is (almost by definition) "eternal," yet it most assuredly begins and ends.

And so on for ever—I fear it would be nugatory, pleonastic (and oh! several other lovely long adjectives!) to try to guard you from these hydra-headed and protean booby-traps; you must tackle them yourself as they arise, and deal with them as best you can: always remembering that often enough you cannot tell which is you and which is the Monkey Puzzle, or who has won. ("Everybody's won; so everybody must have a prize" applies beautifully). And none of it all matters a row of haricots verts sautés; for the conclusion must always be Doubt (see that beastly Book of Lies again—there's a gorgeous chapter about it5)) and the practical moral is this: these contradictions don't occur (or don't matter) in Neschamah.

Also, it might help you quite a lot (by encouraging you when depressed, or amusing you when you want to relax) to read Sir Palamedes the Saracen; Supplement to The Equinox, Vol. I, No. 4. I expect quite a few of his tragi-comic misadventures will be already familiar to you in one disguise or another.

And if the above remarks should embolden you to exclaim: "Perhaps a little drink would do me no great harm" I shall feel that I have deserved well of my country!

For—see Liber Aleph, after Rabelais—the Word of the Last Oracle is TRINC.6)

....

This plaint of yours tails off—and perks up in so doing—with confession of Ambition, and considerations of what you must leave over to your next life. Very right! but all that is covered by your general programme. It is proper to assimilate these ideas with the fundamental structure of your mind: "Perhaps I had better leave 'The Life and opinion of Battling Bill, the Ballarat Bruiser' till, shall we say, six incarnations ahead"—But perhaps you have acquired that already.

No, better still, concentrate on the Next Step! After all, it is the only one you can take, isn't it! Without lust of result, please!

And I shall leave anything else to the next letter.

Love is the law, love under will.

Yours fraternally,

666

LIBER
O
VEL
MANUS
ET
SAGITTAE
SUB FIGURÂ
VI

LIBER O VEL MANVS ET SAGITTAE SVB FIGVR VI

A.'. A.'. Publication in Class B.
Imprimatur:
D.D.S. Praemonstrator
O.S.V. Imperator
N.S.F. Cancellarius

Illustration on page 148: THE SIGNS OF THE GRADES.

These are arranged as ten panels:

These are all halftone photos of a single human in a black Tau robe, barefoot with hood completely closed over the face. The hood displays a six-pointed figure on the forehead—presumably the radiant eye of Horus of the A.'. A.'., but the rendition is

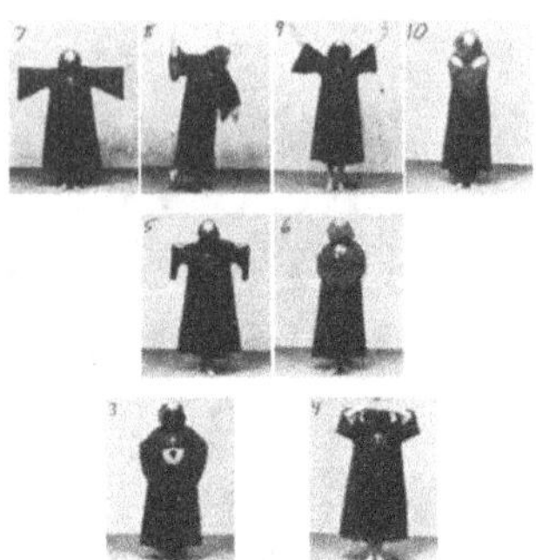

1. Earth: the god Set fighting.
2. Air: The god Shu supporting the sky.
3. Water: the goddess Auramoth.
4. Fire: the goddess Thoum-aesh-neith.

5,6. Spirit: the rending and closing of the veil.

7-10. The L V X signs.

7. + Osiris slain — the cross.
8. L Isis mourning — the Svastica.
9. V Typhon — the Trident.
10. X Osiris risen — the Pentagram.

too poor in detail. There is a cross pendant over the heart. The ten panels are numbered in white in the upper left, but the numerals are very dim even in the Ist edition.

The panels are identified by two columns of numbered captions, 1 to 6 to the left and 7 to 10 to the right. The description is bottom to top and left to right:

"1. Earth—the god Set fighting." Frontal figure. Rt. foot pointed to the fore and angled slightly outward with weight on ball of foot. Lf. heel touching Rt. heel and foot pointed left. Arms form a diagonal with body, right above head and in line with left at waist height. Hands palmer and open with fingers outstretched and together. Head erect.

"2. Air—The god Shu supporting the sky." Frontal. Heels together and slightly angled apart to the front, flat on floor. Head down. Arms angled up on either side of head about head 1.5 ft. from head to wrist and crooked as if supporting a ceiling just at head height with the finger tips. The palms face upward and the backs of the hands away from the head. Thumbs closed to side of palms. Fingers straight and together.

"3. Water—the goddess Auramoth." Same body and foot position as #2, but head erect. Arms are brought down over the chest so that the thumbs touch above the heart and the backs of the hands are to the front. The fingers meet below the heart, forming between thumbs and fingers the descending triangle of water.

"4. Fire—the goddess Thoum-aesh-neith." Frontal. Head and body like #3. Arms are angled so that the thumbs meet in a line over the brow. Palmer side facing. Fingers meet above head, forming between thumbs and fingers the ascending triangle of fire.

"5,6. Spirit—the rending and closing of the veil." Head erect in both. #5 has the same body posture as #1, except that the left and right feet are countercharged and flat on the floor. Arms and hands are crooked forward at shoulder level such that the hands appear to be clawing open a split veil—hands have progressed to a point that the forearms are invisible, being directly pointed at the front. Upper arms are flat and horizontal in the plain of the image. #6. has the same body posture as #1, feet in same position as #1 but flat to the floor. The arms are elbow down against abdomen, with hands forward over heart in claws such that the knuckles are touching. Passing from #5 to #6 or vice versa is done by motion of shoulders and rotation of wrists. This is different from the other sign of opening the veil, the Sign of the Enterer, with is done with hands flat palm to palm and then spread without rotation of wrists.

"7-10. The L V X signs."

"7. + Osiris slain—the cross." Body and feet as in #2. Head bowed. Arms directly horizontal from the shoulders in the plane of the image. Hands with fingers together, thumbs to side of palm and palmer side forward. The tau shape of the robe dominates the image.

"8. L Isis mourning—the Svastica." The body is in semi-profile, head down slightly and facing right of photograph. The arms, hands, legs and feet are positioned to define a swastika. Left foot flat, carrying weight and angled toward the right of the photo. Right foot toe down behind the figure to the left in the photo. Right upper arm due left in photo and forearm vertical with fingers closed and pointing upward. Left arm smoothly canted down to the right of photo, with fingers closed and pointed down.

"9. V Typhon—the Trident." Figure

frontal and standing on tip toe, toes forward and heals not touching. Head back. Arms angled in a "V" with the body to the top and outward in the plain of the photo. Fingers and thumbs as #7, but continuing the lines of the arms.

"10. X Osiris risen—the Pentagram." Body and feet as in #7. Head directly frontal and level. Arms crossed over heart, right over left with hands extended, fingers closed and thumb on side such that the palms rest on the two opposite shoulders.}

I.

1. This book is very easy to misunderstand; readers are asked to use the most minute critical care in the study of it, even as we have done in its preparation.

2. In this book it is spoken of the Sephiroth and the Paths; of Spirits and Conjurations; of Gods, Spheres, Planes, and many other things which may or may not exist.

It is immaterial whether these exist or not. By doing certain things certain results will follow; students are most earnestly warned against attributing objective reality or philosophic validity to any of them.

3. The advantages to be gained from them are chiefly these:

("a") A widening of the horizon of the mind.

("b") An improvement of the control of the mind.

4. The student, if he attains any success in the following practices, will find himself confronted by things (ideas or {13} beings) too glorious or too dreadful to be described. It is essential that he remain the master of all that he beholds, hears or conceives; otherwise he will be the slave of illusion, and the prey of madness.

Before entering upon any of these practices, the student should be in good health, and have attained a fair mastery of Asana, Pranayama and Dharana.

5. There is little danger that any student, however idle or stupid, will fail to get some result; but there is great danger that he will

be led astray, obsessed and overwhelmed by his results, even though it be by those which it is necessary that he should attain. Too often, moreover, he mistaketh the first resting-place for the goal, and taketh off his armour as if he were a victor ere the fight is well begun.

It is desirable that the student should never attach to any result the importance which it at first seems to possess.

6. First, then, let us consider the Book "777" and its use; the preparation of the Place; the use of the Magic Ceremonies; and finally the methods which follow in Chapter V. "Viator in Regnis Arboris," and in Chapter VI. "Sagitta trans Lunam."

II.

1. The student must FIRST obtain a thorough knowledge of "Book 777", especially of columns i., ii., iii., v., vi., vii., ix., xi., xii., xiv., xv., xvi., xvii., xviii., xix., xxxiv., xxxv., xxxviii., xxxix., xl., xli., xlii., xlv., liv., lv., lix., lx., lxi., lxiii., lxx., lxxv., lxxvii., lxviii., lxxix., lxxx., lxxxi., lxxxiii., xcvii., xcviii., xcix., c.,

ci., cxvii., cxviii., cxxxvii., cxxxviii., cxxxix., clxxv., clxxvi., clxxvii., clxxxii.

When these are committed to memory, he will begin to understand the nature of these correspondences.

2. If we take an example, the use of the table will become clear.

Let us suppose that you wish to obtain knowledge of some obscure science.
In column xlv., line 12, you will find "Knowledge of Sciences."

By now looking up line 12 in the other columns, you will find that the Planet corresponding is Mercury, its number eight, its lineal figures the octagon and octagram. The God who rules that planet Thoth, or in Hebrew symbolism Tetragrammaton Adonai and Elohim Tzabaoth, its Archangel Raphael, its Choir of Angels Beni Elohim, its Intelligence Tiriel, its Spirit Taphtatharath, its colours Orange (for Mercury is the Sphere of the Sephira Hod, 8), Yellow, Purple, Grey, and Indigo rayed with Violet; its Magical Weapon the Wand or Caduceus, its Perfumes Mastic and others, its sacred plants Vervain and others, its jewel the Opal or Agate; its sacred animal the Snake, &c., &c.

3. You would then prepare your Place of Working accordingly. In an orange circle you would draw an eight-pointed star of yellow, at whose points you would place eight lamps. The Sigil of the Spirit (which is to be found in Cornelius {15} Agrippa and other books) you would draw in the four colours with such other devices as your experience may suggest.

4. And so on. We cannot here enter at length into all the necessary preparations; and the student will find them fully set forth in the proper books, of which the "Goetia" is perhaps the best example.

These rituals need not be slavishly imitated; on the contrary the student should do nothing the object of which he does not understand; also, if he have any capacity whatever, he will find his own crude rituals more effective than the highly polished ones of other people.

The general purpose of all this preparation is as follows:

5. Since the student is a man surrounded by material objects, if it be his wish to master one particular idea, he must make every material object about him directly suggest that idea. Thus in the ritual quoted, if his glance fall upon the lights, their number suggests Mercury; he smells the perfumes, and again Mercury is brought to his mind. In other words, the whole magical apparatus and ritual is a complex system of mnemonics.

[The importance of these lies principally in the fact that particular sets of images that the student may meet in his wanderings correspond to particular lineal figures, divine names, &c. and are controlled by them. As to the possibility of producing results external to the mind of the seer ("objective," in the ordinary common sense acceptation of the term) we are here silent.]

6. There are three important practices con-

nected with all forms of ceremonial (and the two Methods which later we shall describe). These are: {16}

(1) Assumption of God-forms.

(2) Vibration of Divine Names.

(3) Rituals of "Banishing" and "Invoking".

These, at least, should be completely mastered before the dangerous Methods of Chapters V. and VI. are attempted.

III.

1. The Magical Images of the Gods of Egypt should be made thoroughly familiar. This can be done by studying them in any public museum, or in such books as may be accessible to the student. They should then be carefully painted by him, both from the model and from memory.

2. The student, seated in the "God" position, or in the characteristic attitude of the God desired, should then imagine His image as coinciding with his own body, or as enveloping it. This must be practised until mastery of the image is attained, and an

identity with it and with the God experienced.

It is a matter for very great regret that no simple and certain test of success in this practice exists.

3. The Vibration of God-names. As a further means of identifying the human consciousness with that pure portion of it which man calls by the name of some God, let him act thus:

4. ("a") Stand with arms outstretched.
   ("b") Breathe in deeply through the nostrils, imagining the name of the God desired entering with the breath.
   ("c") Let that name descend slowly from the lungs to the heart, the solar plexus, the navel, the generative organs, and so to the feet. {17}
   ("d") The moment that it appears to touch the feet, quickly advance the left foot about 12 inches, throw forward the body, and let the hands (drawn back to the side of the eyes) shoot out, so that you are standing in the typical position

of the God Horus, ["See" Illustration in Vol. I. No. 1, "Blind Force."] and at the same time imagine the Name as rushing up and through the body, while you breathe it out through the nostrils with the air which has been till then retained in the lungs. All this must be done with all the force of which you are capable. ("e") Then withdraw the left foot, and place the right forefinger upon the lips, so that you are in the characteristic position of the God Harpocrates

5. It is a sign that the student is performing this correctly when a single "Vibration" entirely exhausts his physical strength. It should cause him to grow hot all over, or to perspire violently, and it should so weaken him that he will find it difficult to remain standing.

6. It is a sign of success, though only by the student himself is it perceived, when he hears the name of the God vehemently roared forth, as if by the concourse of ten thousand thunders; and it should appear to

him as if that Great Voice proceeded from the Universe, and not from himself.

In both the above practices all consciousness of anything but the God-form and name should be absolutely blotted out; and the longer it takes for normal perception to return, the better.

IV.

I. The Rituals of the Pentagram and Hexagram must be committed to memory; they are as follows:

The Lesser Ritual of the Pentagram

(i) Touching the forehead say Ateh (Unto Thee).

(ii) Touching the breast say Malkuth (The Kingdom).

(iii) Touching the right shoulder, say ve-Geburah (and the Power).

(iv) Touching the left shoulder, say ve-Gedulah (and the Glory).

(v) Clasping the hands upon the breast, say le-Olahm, Amen (To the Ages, Amen).

(vi) Turning to the East make a pentagram (that of Earth) with the proper weapon (usually the Wand). Say ("i.e." vibrate) I H V H.

(vii) Turning to the South, the same, but say A D N I.

(viii) Turning to the West, the same, but say A H I H.

(ix) Turning to the North, the same, but say A G L A.

Pronounce: Ye-ho-wau, Adonai, Eheieh, Agla.

(x) Extending the arms in the form of a Cross say:

(xi) Before me Raphael;

(xii) Behind me Gabriel;

(xiii) On my right hand Michael.

(xiv) On my left hand Auriel;

(xv) For about me flames the Pentagram,

(xvi) And in the Column stands the six-rayed Star.

(xvii-xxi) Repeat (i) to (v), the Qabalistic Cross.

The Greater Ritual of the Pentagram

The Pentagrams are traced in the air

with the sword or other weapon, the name spoken aloud, and the signs used, as illustrated.

The signs of 2 Degree = 9 Square: Stretch both arms upwards and outwards.

The Pentagrams of Spirit

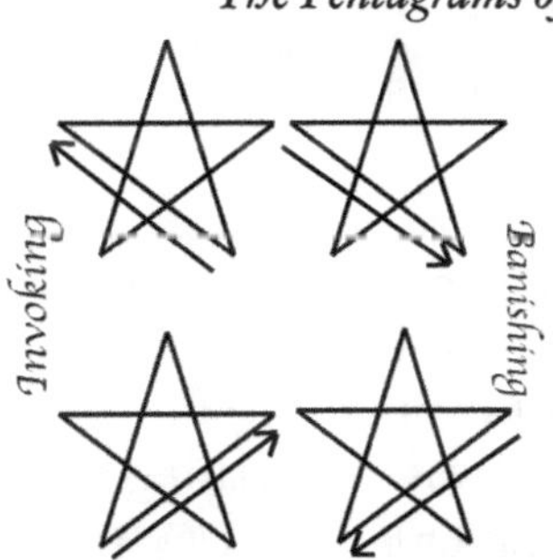

Equilibrium of actives, Name: A H I H (Eheieh).

Equilibrium of passives, Name: A G L A (Agla).

The Signs of the Portal (see illustrations): Extend the hands in front of you, palms outwards, separate them as if in the act of rending asunder a veil or curtain (actives), and then bring them together as if closing it up again and let them fall to the side (passives).

(The Grade of the "Portal" is particularly attributed to the element of Spirit; it refers to the Sun; the Paths of Samekh, Nun and Ayin, are attributed to this degree.

The Pentagrams of Fire

The signs of 4 Degree = 7 Square: Raise the arms above the head and join the hands, so that the tips of the fingers and of the thumbs meet, formulating a triangle (See illustration).

(The Grade of 4 Degree = 7 Square is particularly attributed to the element Fire; it refers to the planet Venus; the paths of Qof, Tzaddi and Peh are attributed to this degree. For other attributions see "777" lines 7 and 31).

The Pentagrams of Water

Name: A L (El).

The signs of 3 Degree = 8 Square: Raise the arms till the elbows are on a level with the shoulders, bring the hands across the chest, touching the thumbs and tips of fingers so as to form a triangle apex downwards (See illustration).

(The Grade of 3 Degree = 8 Square is particularly attributed to the element of Water; it refers to the planet Mercury; the paths of Resh and Shin are attributed to this degree. For other attributions see "777", lines 8 and 23).

The Pentagrams of Air

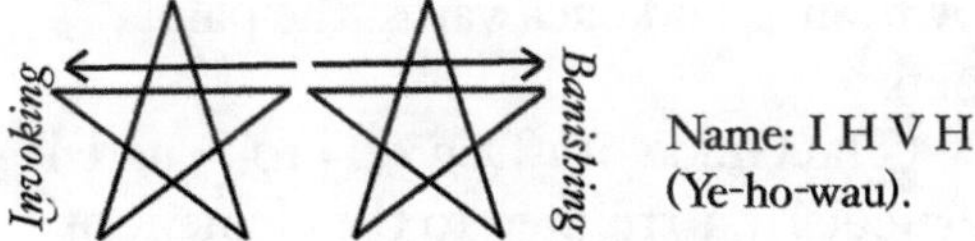

Name: I H V H (Ye-ho-wau).

the elbows bent at right angles, the hands bent back, the palms upwards as if supporting a weight. (See illustration).

(The Grade of 2 Degree = 9 Square is particularly attributed to the element Air; it refers to the Moon; the path of Taw is attributed to this degree. For other attributions see "777" lines 9 and 11).

The Pentagrams of Earth

The Sign of 1 Degree = 10 Square: Advance the right foot, stretch out the right hand upwards and forwards, the left hand downwards and backwards, the palms open.

(The Grade of 1 Degree = 10 Square is particularly attributed to the element of Earth, See "777" lines 10 and 32 bis).

The Lesser Ritual of the Hexagram

This ritual is to be performed after the "Lesser Ritual of the Pentagram".

(i) Stand upright, feet together, left arm at side, right across body, holding the wand or other weapon upright in the median line. Then face East and say:

(ii) I.N.R.I.
Yod. Nun. Resh. Yod.
Virgo, Isis, Mighty Mother.
Scorpio, Apophis, Destroyer.
Sol, Osiris, Slain and Risen.
Isis, Apophis, Osiris, IAO.

(iii) Extend the arms in the form of a cross, and say: "The Sign of Osiris Slain." (See Illustration).

(iv) Raise the right arm to point upwards, keeping the elbow square, and lower the left arm to point downwards, keeping the elbow square, while turning the head over the left shoulder looking down so that the eyes follow the left forearm, and say, "The Sign of the Mourning of Isis." (See Illustration).

(v) Raise the arms at an angle of sixty degrees to each other above the head, which is thrown back, and say, "The Sign of Apophis and Typhon." (See Illustration).

(vi) Cross the arms on the breast, and bow the head and say, "The Sign of Osiris Risen." (See Illustration).

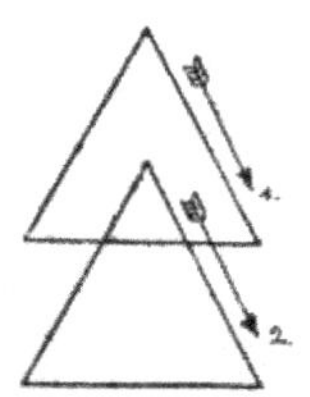

(vii) Extend the arms again as in (iii) and cross them again as in (vi) saying: "L.V.X., Lux, the Light of the Cross".

(viii) With the magical weapon trace the Hexagram of Fire in the East, saying, "Ararita" (Aleph-Resh-Aleph-Resh-Yod-Taw-Aleph).

This Word consists of the initials of a sentence which means "One is His Beginning: One is His Individuality: His Permutation is One."

This hexagram consists of two equilateral triangles, both apices pointed upwards. Begin at the top of the upper triangle and trace it in a dextro-rotary direction. The top of the lower triangle should coincide with the central point of the upper triangle.

(ix) Trace the Hexagram of Earth in the South, saying "ARARITA." This Hexagram has the apex of the lower triangle pointing downwards, and it should be capable of inscription in a circle.

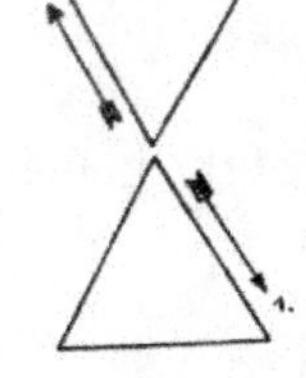

(x) Trace the Hexagram of Air in the West, saying "ARARITA." This Hexagram is like that of Earth; but the bases of the triangles coincide, forming a diamond.

(xi) Trace the hexagram of Water in the North, saying "ARARITA." This hexagram has the lower triangle placed above the upper, so that their apices coincide.

(xii) Repeat (i-vii)

The Banishing Ritual is identical, save that the direction of the Hexagrams must be reversed.

The Greater Ritual of the Hexagram

To invoke or banish planets or zodiacal signs.

The Hexagram of Earth alone is used. Draw the hexagram, beginning from the point which is attributed to the planet you are dealing with. (See "777" col. lxxxiii).

Thus to invoke Jupiter begin from the right-hand point of the lower triangle, dextro-rotary and complete; then trace the upper triangle from its left hand point and complete.

Trace the astrological sigil of the planet in the center of your hexagram.

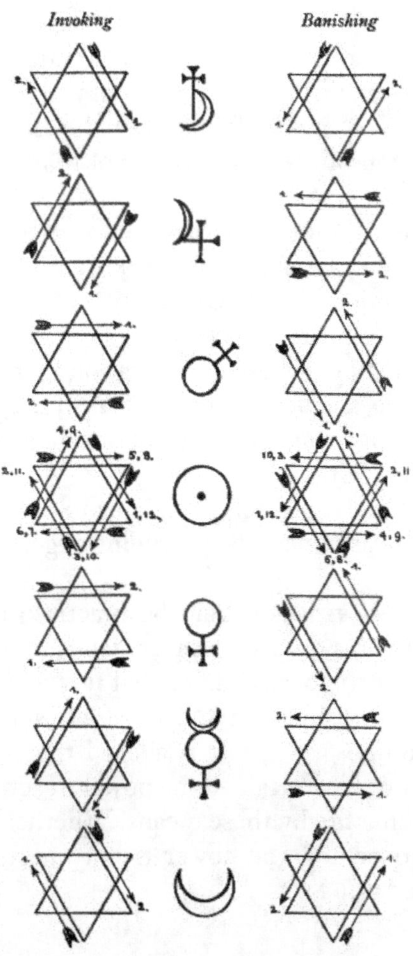
Invoking
Banishing

For the Zodiac use the hexagram of the planet which rules the sign you require ("777", col. cxxxviii); but draw the astrological sigil of the sign, instead of that of the planet.

For Caput and Cauda Draconis use the lunar hexagram, with the sigil of Caput Draconis or Cauda Draconis.

To banish, reverse the hexagram.

In all cases use a conjuration first with Ararita, and next with the name of the God corresponding to the planet or sign you are dealing with.

The Hexagrams pertaining to the planets are as in plate on preceding page.

2. These rituals should be practised until the figures drawn appear in flame, in flame so near to physical flame that it would perhaps be visible to the eyes of a bystander, were one present. It is alleged that some persons have attained the power of actually kindling fire by these means. Whether this be so or not, the power is not one to be aimed at.

3. Success in "banishing" is known by a "feeling of cleanliness" in the atmosphere; success in "invoking" by a "feeling of holiness." It is unfortunate that these terms are so vague.

But at least make sure of this: that any imaginary figure or being shall instantly obey the will of the student, when he uses the appropriate figure. In obstinate cases, the form of the appropriate God may be assumed.

4. The banishing rituals should be used at the commencement of any ceremony whatever. Next, the student should use a general invocation, such as the "Preliminary Invocation" in the "Goetia" as well as a special invocation to suit the nature of his working.

5. Success in these verbal invocations is so subtle a matter, and its grades so delicately shaded, that it must be left to the good sense of the student to decide whether or not he should be satisfied with his result.

V.

1. Let the student be at rest in one of his prescribed positions, having bathed and robed with the proper decorum. Let the place of working be free from all disturbance, and let the preliminary purifications, banishings and invocations be duly accomplished, and, lastly, let the incense be kindled.

2. Let him imagine his own figure (preferably robed in the proper magical garments and armed with the proper magical weapons) as enveloping his physical body, or standing near to and in front of him.

3. Let him then transfer the seat of his consciousness to that imagined figure; so that it may seem to him that he is seeing with its eyes, and hearing with its ears.

This will usually be the great difficulty of the operation.

4. Let him then cause that imagined figure

to rise in the air to a great height above the earth.

5. Let him then stop and look about him. (It is sometimes difficult to open the eyes.)

6. Probably he will see figures approaching him, or become conscious of a landscape.

Let him speak to such figures, and insist upon being answered, using the proper pentagrams and signs, as previously taught.

7. Let him travel about at will, either with or without guidance from such figure or figures.

8. Let him further employ such special invocations as will cause to appear the particular places he may wish to visit.

9. Let him beware of the thousand subtle attacks and deceptions that he will experience, carefully testing the truth of all with whom he speaks.

Thus a hostile being may appear clothed with glory; the appropriate pentagram will in such a case cause him to shrivel or decay.

10. Practice will make the student infinitely wary in these matters.

11. It is usually quite easy to return to the body, but should any difficulty arise, practice (again) will make the imagination fertile. For example, one may create in thought a chariot of fire with white horses, and command the charioteer to drive earthwards.

It might be dangerous to go too far, or to stay too long; for fatigue must be avoided.

The danger spoken of is that of fainting, or of obsession, or of loss of memory or other mental faculty.

12. Finally, let the student cause his imagined body in which he supposes himself to have been travelling to coincide with the physical, tightening his muscles, drawing

in his breath, and putting his forefinger to his lips. Then let him "awake" by a well-defined act of will, and soberly and accurately record his experiences.

It may be added that this apparently complicated experiment is perfectly easy to perform. It is best to learn by "travelling" with a person already experienced in the matter. Two or three experiments will suffice to render the student confident and even expert. See also "The Seer", pp. 295-333.

VI.

1. The previous experiment has little value, and leads to few results of importance. But it is susceptible of a development which merges into a form of Dharana — concentration — and as such may lead to the very highest ends. The principal use of the practice in the last chapter is to familiarise the student with every kind of obstacle and every kind of delusion, so that he may be perfect master of every idea that may arise

in his brain, to dismiss it, to transmute it, to cause it instantly to obey his will.

2. Let him then begin exactly as before, but with the most intense solemnity and determination.

3. Let him be very careful to cause his imaginary body to rise in a line exactly perpendicular to the earth's tangent at the point where his physical body is situated (or to put it more simply, straight upwards).

4. Instead of stopping, let him continue to rise until fatigue almost overcomes him. If he should find that he has stopped without willing to do so, and that figures appear, let him at all costs rise above them.

Yea, though his very life tremble on his lips, let him force his way upward and onward! 5. Let him continue in this so long as the breath of life is in him. Whatever threatens, whatever allures, though it were Typhon and all his hosts loosed from the pit and leagued against him, though it were from the very Throne of God Himself that a Voice issues bidding him stay and be content, let him struggle on, ever on.

6. At last there must come a moment when his whole being is swallowed up in fatigue, overwhelmed by its own inertia.[1]

Let him sink (when no longer can he strive, though his tongue by bitten through with the effort and the blood gush from his nostrils) into the blackness of unconsciousness; and then, on coming to himself, let him write down soberly and accurately a record of all that hath occurred, yea a record of all that hath occurred.

---

1. *This in case of failure. The results of success are so many and wonderful that no effort is here made to describe them. They are classified, tentatively, in the "Herb Dangerious," Part II., "infra".*

ΚΕΦΑΛ ΜF
Buttons and Rosettes
Chapter 46 of *Book of Lies*

The cause of sorrow is the desire of the One to the Many, or of the Many to the One. This also is the cause of joy.

But the desire of one to another is all of sorrow; its birth is hunger, and its death satiety.

The desire of the moth for the star at least saves him satiety.

Hunger thou, O man, for the infinite: be insatiable even for the finite; thus at The End shalt thou devour the finite, and become the infinite.

Be thou more greedy that the shark, more full of yearning than the wind among the pines.

The weary pilgrim struggles on; the satiated pilgrim stops.

The road winds uphill: all law, all nature must be overcome.

Do this by virtue of THAT in thyself before which law and nature are but shadows.

666

Blood-Soaked Buddha/Hard Earth Pascal
by Noah Cicero

"What if you had to live for eternity with your current shitty attitude?"

Marking a significant departure from Cicero's fictional and poetic works, *Blood-Soaked Buddha/Hard Earth Pascal* is a lucid philosophical treatise. Rather than entertain dogma, Cicero approaches a discussion of Buddhism from the refreshing perspective of the everyman, providing a profound spiritual analysis as well as a sharp critique of capitalism. There are even some pretty good ghost stories.

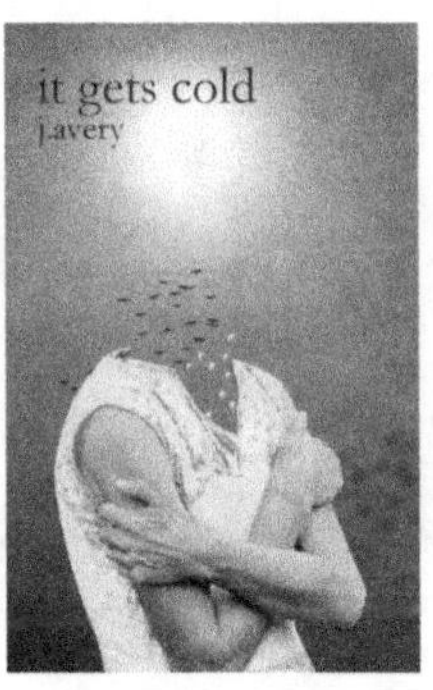

it gets cold
by jasper avery

---

it gets cold demands a body that is both the haunting and the house, a queerness that is both living and dying. What can be gained by inhabiting this liminal space? What can the inhabitation of dying bring to the living? What can be done when it gets cold?

Major Diamonds Nights & Knives
by Katie Foster

Major Diamonds Nights & Knives is a poetry project modeled after a deck of cards. While writing this poem, Katie Foster felt possessed by a spirit who died in childbirth. She tried to tell her story as best she could.

Cactus
by Nathaniel Kennon Perkins

“Shades of Updike’s ‘A&P’ but much less boring.” - Bart Schaneman, author of *The Silence is the Noise*

“Goddamn good.” - Adam Gnade, author of *the Do-It-Yourself Guide to Fighting the Big Motherfuckin’ Sad*

“Perkins does what classic literature does. He invites you to witness an accident, and like the desert, it is beautiful.”
- Noah Cicero, author of *Nature Documentary*

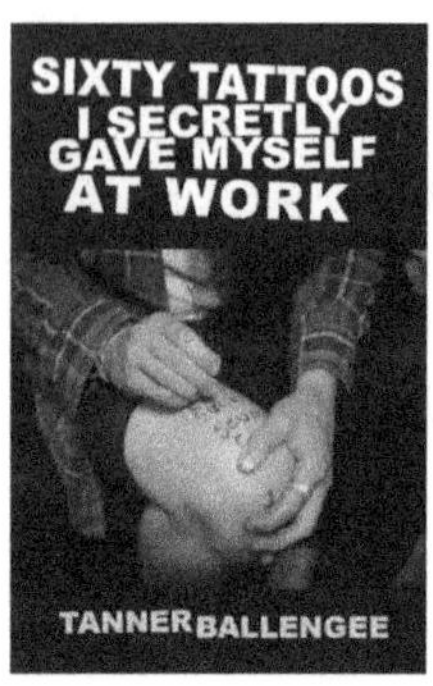

Sixty Tattoos I Secretly Gave Myself at Work
by Tanner Ballengee

Ex-girlfriends. LSD. Motorcycle and canoe trips. *Sienfeld*. Skateboarding. Drunk friends and punk rock and shitty jobs. *Sixty Tattoos I Secretly Gave Myselt at Work* is the most beautiful, the most vulnerable of punk and adventure memoirs. Each vignette centers around a hand-poked tattoo that the author gave himself on company time.

The Pocket Peter Kropotkin

Collected in this cute, pocket-sized volume are eight of Kropotkin's essays. The book starts with his indispensable article on anarchism, originally written for the Eleventh Edition of the *Encyclopedia Britannica*, and moves forward to expound on his ideas, which include prison abolition, syndicalism, expropriation, etc.

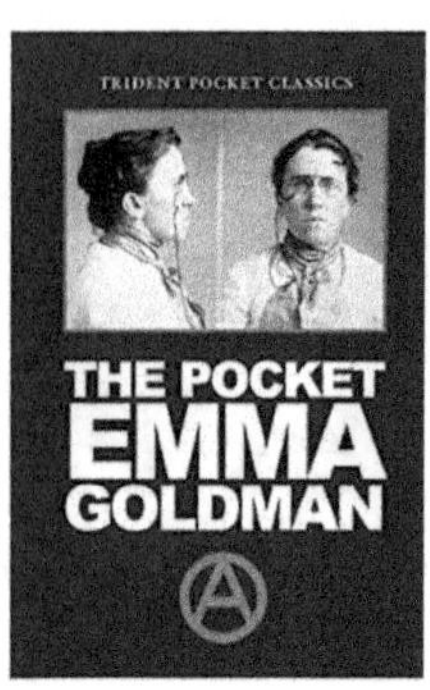

The Pocket Emma Goldman

"I may be arrested, I may be tried and thrown into jail, but I never will be silent; I never will acquiesce or submit to authority, nor will I make peace with a system which degrades woman to a mere incubator and which fattens her on innocent victims. I now and here declare war upon this system..."

Some great Goldman essays collected in one place. This book is perfect for carrying in your pocket so you can secretly read anarcha-feminist literature while you're supposed to be working.

The Silence is the Noise
by Bart Schaneman

After a few years living in cities, Ethan Thomas returns to his rural Nebraska hometown and takes a reporting job at the community newspaper. He stumbles upon a big story when an out-of-state oil company pumps enough fracking wastewater into the ground to induce earthquakes. As Ethan learns to write he reconnects with a young woman from his childhood. This is a story about the complicated relationship we have with the places we know best, the pull of the outside world, and finding something to love.